Extraordinary Leadership

Other Business Books by Cher & Bil Holton

The Manager's Short Course to a Long Career: 101 Proven Techniques to Accelerate Your Managerial Worth

Living at the Speed of Life: Staying in Control in a World Gone Bonkers!

Suppose ... Questions to Turbo-Charge Your Business and Your Life

From Ballroom to Bottom Line ... in business and in life

Crackerjack Choices: 200 of the Best Choices You Will Ever Make

Seriously? 25 Cringe-Worthy Phrases Leaders Use That Rob Them of Their Credibility ... and How to Retool Them

Anthologies created and edited by Cher & Bil Holton:

Rekindling the Human Spirit: An Anthology of Hope, Courage, and Inspiration (Foreword by Jamie Valvano Howard, daughter of legendary NCSU basketball coach Jim Valvano, honoring his legacy of hope, courage, and inspiration)

That's My Story and I'm Sticking to It! An Anthology of Stories to Inspire, Encourage, and Enjoy (Foreword by world explorer and adventurer John Goddard)

Life, Work, and Money ~ From a Woman's Perspective: An Anthology of Life Lessons From the Hearts and Minds of Women (Foreword by Kay Yow, former Head Coach, NCSU Women's Basketball Team)

Extraordinary Leadership

*Connecting With Your Seven Core Abilities to
Bring Out the Extraordinary Abilities in Others*

Cher Holton, Ph.D.

Copyright ©2018 Cher Holton
All rights reserved.

First Edition

Reproduction or translation of any part of this work beyond that permitted by Section 107 or 108 of the 1976 United States Copyright Act without the permission of the copyright owner is unlawful.
Requests for permission or further information should be addressed to the authors, c/o Liberty Publishing Group 1405 Autumn Ridge Drive, Durham. NC 27712.

For information about special discounts for bulk purchases, please contact the authors through their website: holtonconsulting.com

Library of Congress Cataloging-in-Publication Data

Holton, Cher, 1950-

Extraordinary Leadership : Connecting with your seven core abilities to bring out the extraordinary abilities in others / Cher Holton
p. cm.

ISBN 978-1-893095-97-7

1. Leadership   2. Business   3. Personal Development
I. Cher Holton   II. Title

Library of Congress Control Number: 2018903403

Book cover and interior design: Cher Holton
Research: Bil Holton, Ph.D.

Dedicated to Bil, my incredible husband, business partner, dance partner, and definitely "my person," without whom I would never be the person I am ~

and to Ray Miklos, the best manager I ever had—an amazing leader who taught me more about leadership in the four years I worked for him than I learned in any class I ever took, any book I ever read, or from any other leader I ever experienced.

When leaders lead from the highest levels of their Core Abilities, people will respond in extraordinary ways!

(Cher Holton)

Table of Contents

Introduction 1
Your Seven Core Abilities
    Authentegrity 25
    Intuitive Wisdom 47
    Inner Strength 69
    Questioning Unquestioned Answers 87
    Optimistic Spirit 109
    Self-Reliance 127
    Mentoring Mindset 145
Appendix: Maximizing Your Core Abilities 163
Acknowledgments/Photo Credits 169
Endnotes 171
About the Author 179
Index 181

Introduction

All leaders want to believe that deep within their souls there is a very special reason they are in leadership positions, that they have something valuable to contribute to the world, that they have a special purpose, that they are contributing to their organization through their leadership experiences. They also have a sense for the kind of lives they'd like to live and a desire to find the right kinds of opportunities which suit their talents and aspirations. And you can be sure that their colleagues and employees feel the same way.

Yet for far too many leaders, those inner promptings and ardent hopes have become detoured by the frustrations and lost opportunities associated with the daily grind of work expectations. Many leaders have given up on what they thought they could be. Hundreds have settled for ordinariness, or succumbed to the weariness and stress of the job. Hundreds more hold onto their dreams but fail to take the necessary steps to make those dreams real. To the extent this may describe you or the people you manage, let the portions of this book that speak to you be your call to action.

Psychologists have told us that we can't completely separate our personal lives from our work lives. We carry residues of our unrealized dreams, our frustrations and lost opportunities, and our negative self-concepts with us to work. All of our life experience, in one form or another, accompanies us to the office, to the work floor, to the board room. It impacts the way we show up as leaders, and seeps into every leadership action we take.

When we get busy at work, the deeper parts of us may seem to go away for a while by slipping into our subconsciousness—but guess what? These deeper parts are still there! Our effectiveness as leaders depends on how well we're able to manage our human vulnerabilities and virtues as we lead, and that depends on our state of mind, our self-discipline, our commitment and focus to the work at hand. This determines how engaged or disengaged we are as we lead, which in turn determines how engaged or disengaged our empoyees will be. Luckily, you have incredible Core Abilities within you that guarantee your being able to become an Extraordinary Leader.

In this highly innovative leadership book, you'll discover guaranteed prescriptions to help you, as a leader, achieve the productivity, engagement, teamwork, and results you deserve by transforming yourself into an Extraordinary Leader—because you have aligned yourself with your Core Nature.

I guarantee more employee engagement as a result of your enrollment in the prescriptions I present. Why am I so confident—and enthusiastic? Because the type of engagement I'm offering is the genuine convergence of both your extraordinary qualities and the extraordinary qualities of those who work for you. And I've got the science to prove it!

Your Core Nature is 'The Extraordinary You' waiting to be released, allowing you to become an Extraordinary Leader.

The material in this book is grounded in the sciences of positive psychology, neuroscience, quantum physics, sociology, and positivity. I believe that including scientific research adds depth and credibility to the leadership theories and practices I provide, and creates an easy-to-understand guide for the practical application and use of the seven Core Abilities that can literally transform you and the people who work for you. The symphony of productivity that results from an engaged environment is extraordinary! I've seen it! Leaders who establish a climate of genuine and sustained employee engagement enjoy the benefits of leading involved and dedicated employees. Employees who feel valued for their talents and contributions will drive themselves toward unbelievable excellence. I've seen that too!

Introduction

Unfortunately, in many cases organizations have not discovered the key for honest and sustained employee engagement. Consider the latest Gallop Poll statistics:

> A new Gallup poll finds that 52% of all full-time workers in America aren't involved in, enthusiastic about or committed to their work. Another 18% are 'actively disengaged,' meaning they have gone beyond just checking out mentally, emotionally, and physically. That leaves just 30% of American workers who feel excited about their jobs.

That's an amazing set of statistics! You might want to compare your experience with what these numbers say. It's not for lack of leadership training ... there is a plethora of programs focusing on leadership! But something seems to still be missing, which is why this book remains a cut above traditional leadership and employee engagement programs. Traditional leadership development and employee engagement strategies, in and of themselves, are not the panacea for sustainable growth. Conventional practices such as open communication; job performance clarity and timely feedback; nurturing organizational culture; wellness and productivity programs; well-managed rewards and recognition systems; on-site day care and exercise rooms; amicable and respectful relationships between managers, peers, and hourly employees; career development opportunities; employee retention strategies; flexible work hours; and management transparency are all beneficial, but not sufficient to ensure sustainable employee engagement.

Most traditional employee engagement strategies are based on extrinsic incentives and rewards which work for a while, but then lose their luster. I call these strategies **e-Engagement**. In fact, most e-Engagement strategies will get people to work, and will even serve as initial motivators in order to maintain a certain life style level; however, once that level is obtained, e-Engagement techniques will have little impact on inspiring the higher levels of behavior we desire from employees (such as initiative, creativity, innovation, commitment, and accountability).

For these high qualities, leaders need a different strategy—an intrinsic employee engagement I call **i-Engagement**. And it begins with looking at yourself! Too many bright, conscientious, talented leaders get so caught up in material success and ego pursuits (extrinsic incentives) that they neglect the one thing that will make them effective, productive, and successful leaders: connecting with their Core Nature, the deeper part of them that is the seat of their higher functioning, their phenomenal abilities, their incredible uniqueness, their realized potential! This is the ultimate intrinsic reward. Their Core Nature is that extraordinary part of them waiting to be released!

From my experience, leaders will not achieve what they want to achieve, be what they want to be, and do what they believe they are put here to do until they make this connection—the connection with their Core Nature. Once that connection is made, all the rest of their lives falls into place.

It just makes good business sense to get in touch with your deeper, more positively oriented self—The Extraordinary You.

I invite you to enjoy the experience of discovering your extraordinary nature and leading a team of truly engaged employees. I believe you have what it takes to nurture the deeper, more optimistic nature that's inherent in you and in all of your people. As a work and life enrichment impact consultant, that's my forte—helping you cultivate your Extraordinary Leadership abilities so you can help your people think and be more positive and engaged as they express their extraordinary abilities.

Here's my guarantee: Using the strategies outlined in this book *will* help you develop into an Extraordinary Leader—a leader who builds a team of people who feel good about themselves, recognize their skills and talents, and work together to be more productive and less complaining, more enthusiastic and less pessimistic, more engaged and less distracted, more positive and less moody, more present and less absent. And you will see that reflected in your bottom line with increased profitability, market share sustainability, and happier, more committed, totally engaged employees.

No matter where you are in life, you want more of the things that you believe will make you happy, healthy, productive, and fulfilled. It doesn't matter how well you are already doing, or aren't; how prosperous you already are, or not; how professionally fulfilled you are, or not; how financially stable you are, or aren't—you have the choice of making the all important connection with the Extraordinary You, your Deeper Self, your Core Nature.

Making that choice is the difference between your leadership success and feeling that you're in the wrong career. It's the difference between feeling fulfilled and wondering if you'll ever achieve anything worthwhile. It's the difference between the current you and the leader you'd like to be.

A Quick Exercise of "Futuring"

Let's take a quick look back to the year 2001. What was going on?

- George W. Bush was sworn in as the 43rd President of the United States
- NASCAR legend Dale Earnhardt died in a last lap crash in the Daytona 500
- Apple announced iTunes at the MacWorld Expo in San Francisco
- Wikipedia, a free Wiki content encyclopedia, went online and became "THE" source of information
- Millionaire Dennis Tito became the world's first civilian space tourist
- The Human Genome Sequence was revealed
- The Arizona Diamondbacks defeated the heavily-favored New York Yankees in seven games to win their first World Series
- 32 year-old Erik Weihenmayer, of Boulder, Colorado, became the first sight-challenged person to reach the summit of Mount Everest
- Enron filed for Chapter 11 bankruptcy

- Apple released the iPod and Microsoft followed with the release of Windows XP
- Noah, a gaur (Southeast Asian ox), was born, and was the first animal of an endangered species to be cloned
- The Leaning Tower of Pisa reopened to the tune of $27,000,000 to fortify it without fixing its famous lean
- On June 6th, Sasha Obama was born. She was the daughter of Barack Obama and Michelle Obama, who would later become the 44th President (and first African-American President) and the First Lady.
- Almost 3,000 people were killed in suicide attacks on September 11th at the World Trade Center in New York, the Pentagon in Arlington, Virginia, and in rural Shanksville, Pennsylvania

The year 2001 was certainly a year to remember. Think for a moment. Where were you then? What were you doing? What were you like? How old were you? Who were your friends? What were your hopes and dreams? How did these events change your perspective about the world—about yourself?

What if someone had asked you then, "Where will you be twenty years from now?"—"What will you be doing?"—"What kind of career will you have?" "What will be your greatest accomplishments?" How would you have answered them?

Are you where you thought you'd be today? Have you accomplished what you thought you would? What is important to you now? Looking at your own life, what major personal and/or professional experiences have shaped your life over the last fifteen to twenty years? How many of the goals you have set over this time period have you actually accomplished? Have you discovered your life purpose yet? Are you the leader you thought you would be? Have you fulfilled your highest potential? Who is the real you?

There's one thing the answers to these questions have in common: They all depend on the extent to which you've connected with what neuroscientists refer to as your Deeper Self and to what I call the Extraordinary You. This book will help you make that connection even stronger, and allow you to become an Extraordinary Leader.

Understanding Your Core Nature

"Know thyself" is an ancient Greek aphorism that was inscribed in the forecourt of the Temple of Apollo at Delphi. It has been used throughout history as an injunction for all of us to take getting to know ourselves seriously. There are a growing number of leaders who have taken the injunction seriously and have achieved the health, wealth, and happiness they sought. I believe that when each of us gets *us* right, our world will be right. The us, of course, is the Extraordinary Us, the us we discover when we are aligned with our Core Nature.

Your Core Nature is the foundation of your being. It is the wise you; the resourceful you; the you who has all of the answers; the you who has the strength to lift a car off a loved one; the you who has the ability to memorize a series of 500 numbers in their exact order; the you who can survive stage four cancer and go on to live a healthy, happy life; the you who can break cinder blocks with your bare hand; the you who can discover the innovative solution to a business issue; the you who knows how to create an environment conducive to engagement, productivity, and growth.

Your Core Nature is real. Philosophers and spiritual leaders have referred to it. But so have psychologists and sociologists. Psychologist D. W. Winnicott coined the term "True Self" in 1960 to describe a "sense of self based on spontaneous authentic experience, a sense of all-out personal aliveness" or "feeling real." Psychologist Alice Miller agrees and says that when the 'True Self' is liberated it "emerges like a butterfly liberated from its chrysalis and an unexpected wealth of vitality is released." Psychologist Carl Rogers also referred to it as the True Self. Psychologist Daniel Stern calls it the Core Self; Psychoanalyst Eric Fromm called it the Original Self; neuroscientist Andrew Newberg refers to it as our Deeper Self. I call it our Core Nature—the "Extraordinary You!"

We all have that 'Self' psychologists, neuroscientists, and psychoanalysts talk about. You have it. Your colleagues have it. Your direct reports have it. Your customers and suppliers have it. Your key stakeholders have it.

Try reading the next paragraph out loud ... as you look at yourself in the mirror. Try replacing "you" with "me."

I believe in the Extraordinary You, the Wise You, the Spectacular You, the Authentic You, the Phenomenal You, the Peerless You, the Exceptional You, the Unparalleled You, the Legendary You, the Marvelous You, the One-of-a-Kind You, the Remarkable You, the Awesome You, the Astounding You, the Stunning You, the Electrifying You, the Sensational You, the Mesmerizing You, the Amazing You, the Spellbinding You, the Hypnotic You, the Fascinating You, the Fantabulous You, the Stupendous You, the Jaw-Dropping You, the Mind-Boggling You, the Dazzling You, the Brilliant You.

If it sounds like I'm going over-board with those descriptions, I invite you to think for a moment about how much of your hidden potential goes unnoticed. I encourage you to think about leaders you admire who have done extraordinary things. And I certainly hope you'll research people who have amazing talents and abilities, who have pushed the limits of human capacity. The world is full of individuals who have expressed their extraordinary nature in one area or another.

You have an *Extraordinary You* hiding within you that is just waiting to be expressed. Your employees and colleagues have an "Extraordinary Nature" that's just waiting to be expressed, as do your customers, suppliers, and contractors. As an Extraordinary Leader, you have the privilege and responsibility to cultivate this core nature within those who work for you and with you, and bring out their Extraordinary Nature too.

A Quick Peek at the Science

The underlying goal of this book to help leaders connect with their extraordinary nature. It is a hero's journey. It is a 'work-in-progress' personal journey of introspection, self-discovery (improving the everyday you), and Self-recovery (becoming consciously one with your Core Nature—the Extraordinary You, the Wise You, the Spectacular You, the Authentic You, the Fantabulous You, your Deeper Self ... you get the point). But even more, research has proven that when people are able to work in an environment that reinforces their extraordinary nature, amazing things happen!

According to a study reported in *Personnel Psychology*, there are strong correlations between employee engagement and desirable business outcomes such as retention of talent, customer service, individual performance, team performance, business unit productivity, and even enterprise-level financial performance.[1]

Throughout this book, I will be citing various quotes, research findings, and relevant supporting data drawn from a variety of scientific fields. I felt it might be helpful to give you a quick peek at the major sciences I've included, so you recognize my approach is evidence-based and research-supported.

Positive Psychology is a recent branch of psychology whose purpose was summed up by Martin Seligman and Mihaly Csikszentmihalyi in the following statement: "We believe that a psychology of positive human functioning will arise, which achieves a scientific understanding and effective interventions to build thriving individuals, families, and communities." Positive psychologists seek "to find and nurture genius and talent," and "to make normal life more fulfilling," and not simply to treat mental illness.[2]

The current research in Positive Psychology supports my belief that you can, indeed, create a work environment that is conducive to employee engagement—that supports a strong work ethic, enhanced profits, and strengthened commitment to customer satisfacation—while at the same time allowing employees to be enriched and encouraged to use their strengths and talents to the fullest. Throughout this book, I quote various research findings and thoughts expressed by scientists in this field, to help clarify the incredible impact the development of the seven Core Abilities can have in your organization and in the lives of every person working with you.

Neuroscience is the scientific study of the nervous system. Traditionally, neuroscience was seen as a branch of biology; however, it is currently viewed as an interdisciplinary science which collaborates with other fields such as chemistry, biology, engineering, linguistics, mathematics, medicine, computer science, philosophy, physics, and psychology. There is an incredible amount of research related to the brain, nervous system, and behavior which directly impacts how we can work more effectively and tap into our seven Core Abilities.

And More . . . Other major sources of our work include the neuro-scientific work of Dr. Andrew Newberg, Associate Professor in the Department of Radiology and Psychiatry, University of Pennsylvania; the Positivity research of Dr. Barbara Fredrickson, Kenan Distinguished Professor of Psychology and Principal Investigator of the Positive Emotions and Psychophysiology Lab at the University of North Carolina; the happiness studies presented by psychology professor Sonja Lyubomirsky, University of California, Riverside, Stanford University; research by neuropsychologist Rick Hanson, co-founder of the Wellspring Institute for Neuroscience and Contemplative Wisdom; physicist Paul Davies, Director of the Beyond Center, Arizona State University; astrophysicist, Bernard Haisch, former Deputy Director of the Center for Extreme Ultraviolate Astrophysics at U.C. Berkeley; cell biologist Bruce Lipton, former researcher at Stanford University's School of Medicine; and Michael S. Gazzaniga, Professor of Psychology at the University of California, Santa Barbara. It also includes the lastest employee engagement books, studies, and best practices captured from my research. But be aware

Introduction

that even as the ink was drying on this publication, there were already new books and articles coming out.

One thing I know for sure—every circumstance invites you to be who you are at your Core. Every situation demands your true colors. Each challenge you face requires you to think, choose, and act from the truth of who you really are.

I can categorically tell you from personal experience and from a thorough investigation of the last fifty years of human potential research that when your "ordinary self" (the everyday you) is aligned with your Deeper Self (the Extraordinary You), you can meet any human challenge with grace and poise. You can achieve things you thought were impossible. You can most assuredly find the happiness, success, prosperity, and sense of inner peace you seek. It will come as no surprise to you that this applies to those who work with you, too.

> According to the latest research in the neurosciences, Dr. Andrew Newberg asserts, "Beneath the mind's perception of thoughts, memories, emotions, and beneath the subjective awareness we think of as the self, there is a Deeper Self, a state of pure awareness that sees beyond the limits of subject and object, and rests in a universe where all things are one." [3]

People who have aligned themselves with their Deeper Self, their Extraordinary Nature, recognize they have unlimited potential that can be tapped, a potential within them in the form of their Extraordinary Self. They also become aware that they have seven Core Abilities that make it possible for them to connect with their Core Nature at the deepest, most powerful level.

The good news is that all of us possess these Core Abilities; However, many leaders do not draw upon those qualities, making their work more difficult and less fulfilling. These exceptional qualities lie dormant within most people, and remain either unused, under-used, ineffectively over-used, or repressed.

Research has uncovered this telling truth: *Nothing worthwhile has ever been achieved except by those who dared believe that 'something' deep inside of them was superior to anything they were going through.* It is a belief, a feeling of certainty about something that can be accomplished in our lives despite the rantings of naysayers who say it cannot be done. It's a compelling urge within ourselves that proclaims it is us who determines our success or failure and not outer circumstances.

I nicknamed it the *Bannister Effect*, after the Englishman Roger Bannister, who was the first to run a sub-four minute mile. Sports authorities and physiologists said it couldn't be done. Roger proved them wrong by running a 3.59.4 second mile at Iffley Road Track in Oxford. And once he proved it could, indeed, be achieved, many others were able to replicate it!

Accessing—and then expressing—these qualities begins with a belief that you are endowed with extraordinary potential, and that you can see that potential in others. Drawing out that potential is the key to sustained—and profitable—employee engagement—and that is exactly what this book is all about!

Once you have connected with your Core Abilities as a leader, you'll be prepared to mentor your employees, leading them through this same seven-chapter process. It will help them understand, connect with, and put into practice the seven Core Abilities that lead to an engaged workplace. You can choose the timeframe based on your specific situation; however, we recommend the process be completed in no less than seven weeks (where you would be meeting with your employees once a week, addressing a new Core Ability each week) and no longer than seven months (where you would be meeting with your employees once a month, with each month addressing a new Core Ability).

Introduction

Understanding the Layout of This Book

This Extraordinary Leadership book is designed to help you believe in and develop your own uniqueness first, realizing, of course, that those who work with and for you are unique as well. It is designed so you can connect with your own Core Abilities, then create an on-going discussion with your employees to build an environment conducive to employee engagement by helping everyone recognize and connect with their own "Extraodinary Nature." As you guide your team in understanding and developing their seven Core Abilities, you will experience improved communication among team members, increased initiative and cooperation, heightened productivity, and an incredible sense of engagement among your people—at all levels—both internally and with customers/clients/venders.

The book is divided into seven chapters following this Introduction, each of which focuses on one of the Seven Core Abilities you possess that, when cultivated, will transform you into an Extraordinary Leader. Each chapter includes:

- a detailed description of the Core Ability, with its impact on your leadership effectiveness,
- the science and research supporting this Core Ability;
- tips on how to strengthen the Core Ability;
- a summary of the Core Ability and it's corresponding color, and how color can help integrate the connection with and use of the Core Ability;
- two strategies designed to help you use the Core Ability at its highest, most elevated level of expression (Laser Focus Technique and Self-Directed Activity);
- a Personal Reflection Page to capture your experiences.

According to social psychologists, self-awareness and self-reflection provide the emotional insights to identify and improve upon personal and professional areas of improvement while capitalizing on strengths and special abilities.[4]

Imagine how a high level of employee engagement would look in a work environment that encourages its employees, at all levels, to express their more optimistic, more creative, more decisive, more authentic selves! The good news is it doesn't take expensive external incentives to achieve sustained employee engagement.

All it requires is a work environment that helps people connect with seven Core Abilities they already have, but rarely use to the degree they could if they knew they possessed them and understood how to access them.

A Quick Self Check

(Tip – There are no right answers, just honest ones):

1. What are my greatest strengths as a leader?

2. What was one situation where my leadership ability did not work as well as I would have liked? What went wrong?

3. How would my employees describe me?

4. Am I more comfortable with rules and regulations, or flexibility and creativity?

5. How do I handle pressure and uncertainty?

6. How do I deal with employees who exhibit difficult behaviors or challenge my authority?

Introduction

The Seven Core Abilities and Their Colors

Here is a quick snapshot of each of the Core Abilities to help you realize you—and your people—have these qualities and everyone can develop them to fully realize the incredible potential that can be unleashed in your work environment.

I have included a color to represent each Core Ability, because research has shown that color can affect our brain in different ways, enhancing our learning experience and helping us be more productive, less stressed, and more creative.[5] At the end of each chapter, you will find ideas on ways to use color to enhance the connection to the Core Ability.

The seven Core Abilities that Extraordinary Leaders have in common are:

- Authentegrity (Red)
- Intuitive Wisdom (Yellow)
- Inner Strength (Russet)
- Questioning Unquestioned Answers (Blue)
- Optimistic Spirit (Orange)
- Self-Reliance (Purple)
- Mentoring Mindset (Green)

I hope you're thinking to yourself: *I already have those qualities within me, to some extent ... and so do my top performers!* That's good, because it's true. In fact, everyone has these qualities and is expressing them at varying degrees. The two questions I'm going to ask are:

- How often do you *consciously* use these qualities?
- How serious are you about developing them, so you can use them at a deeper, more intentional level?

You will be surprised at how much of the 'potential you' is still tucked away deep within you. I can tell you, without one moment's hesitation, that when you get serious about developing each of these phenomenal qualities, you will become one with your Core Nature and fulfill your incredible potential as a leader. And the amount of influence you'll have on those around you will encourage them to follow your lead. The result—take a moment right now to visualize how this would look to you:

***Extraordinary Leaders ... Extraordinary Employees ...
Working Together for Extraordinary Results!***

Introduction

The Truth About Sustainable Employee Engagement

Before you jump into this "Extraordinary" material (hope you don't get tired of that word), I'd like to pause for a moment to share a little research and insight into the whole idea of employee engagement. If you've been in management for any time at all, you know that traditional forms of engagement strategies work initially but then seem to lose their appeal over the long haul. Why? Because the traditional forms of engagement are not engagement at all! They are merely enrollment. The same thing holds true for sustainable employee engagement today as it did 125 years ago for motivating employees—*you can't make people motivated or engaged if they don't want to be motivated or engaged!* Psychologists have told us that for decades.[6]

Having said that, you can be sure there are things you can do to help foster genuine employee engagement. You can create an environment that cultivates engagement so people perform work tasks because they enjoy the assigned work tasks, rather than simply *doing* their jobs for fear of *losing* their jobs.

If I was going to offer you traditional employee engagement tactics, there would be no use in developing this *Extraordinary Leadership* book. You are, no doubt, already very well acquainted with thousands of conventional employee motivational and employee retention practices which have been around for years. These well-worn employee engagement strategies, in and of themselves, are valuable; however, they are not the panacea for sustainable growth. They may work for awhile, but they will not guarantee sustained employee engagement.

The conventional practices outlined earlier in the Introduction have slipped in their effectiveness to keep employees engaged. Extrinsic forms of motivation (material things) have become prerequisites and givens. They may attract top performers but not keep them. **It is the intrinsic motivators that will guarantee lasting engagement.**

Employees who are fully involved in, and enthusiastic about their work, will act in ways that further their organization's interests. You are very aware that engagement is the degree of employees' positive emotional attachment to their job, colleagues, managers, customers, and organization that profoundly influences their willingness to learn and perform at work. This level of immersion, as you know, is distinctively different from traditional employee satisfaction, motivation, and organizational cultures.

Here's what the research says about the clues that indicate there's a problem brewing (and don't forget to check yourself out too!):

1. *Mood Changes:* Your once vibrant employees begin to resemble ... zombies. Simply having unmotivated employees in the workplace is often enough to affect the moods and productivity of other employees. Often, a sudden change in an employee's mood signal's something is brewing. If this goes unnoticed, employees may feel as if they don't matter.
2. *Weariness, fatigue, and lethargy:* When employees are no longer eager to complete tasks, something has caused their excitement about work to evaporate. They spend more time in meetings gossiping than they do involved in their work assignments.
3. *Increase in absences:* When certain employees who normally have a good record of attendance begin calling in sick or requesting personal leave more often than usual, your red flags should be rising. This is often a sign of either personal issues that are affecting the job, or as is often the case, it is a sign of disinterest, withdrawal, and disengagement.
4. *Complaints and Criticisms:* One of the final and most blatant signs of disengagement is outright complaining and unwarranted criticism about anything and everything: policies, work schedules, work environment, the parking lot, customers, coworkers, managers, and anything else they can think of to cause friction and dissention. Pay attention to "water-cooler conversations!" If you hear employees complaining about issues around your workplace, it could mean they're dissatisfied and they feel that the company's goals and values are not in line with their own goals and values. **Nothing is more infectious and damaging to employee spirit than contagious disengagement.**[7]

Introduction

I've seen these symptoms repeated in the workplace many times, and I'll bet you have too. What happens is that external motivators—like most employee engagement programs—lose their shine. They are extrinsic motivators that work over the short run but do not have a lasting influence.

Employers have spent nearly a billion dollars on employee engagement in the past year, and current research is projecting that number will easily rise to $1.5 billion. The 1.5 billion dollar question is: What are employers getting for this investment? Not much, if you accept the findings in the most recent Gallup report, *State of the American Workplace.*

The statistics on the level of employee engagement have virtually flat-lined, with about 30% of employees genuinely engaged since the initial Gallup reports in the late 1990's. So, the percentage of engaged employees has not improved at all in the last twenty-five years!

No amount of spending or energy devoted to extrinsic engagement strategies is likely to dramatically affect employee engagement unless people recognize that employee engagement, as it is currently being practiced, puts the burden for engagement on the employer and leaves employees to judge whether or not they want to be genuinely engaged. It goes way beyond whether an employee is "feeling happy" on the job. True engagement comes when leaders treat employees as key stakeholders in the business. That's where Extraordinary Leadership comes into the mix! Extraordinary Leaders know how to skillfully tip the balance of responsibility to each employee to be engaged.

Here's a powerful piece of the puzzle: employees must do their part! Employee engagement is a partnership. Employees need to recognize that both they and their employers are in the engagement business. Each has a role to play to make the workplace conducive to performance, productivity, and profits.[8]

The question employees, at all levels within the organization, must ask is this:

Am I getting out of bed each workday morning and heading in to engage in something that is worth my time and effort?

If the answer to that question is 'yes,' then investing in both intrinsic and extrinsic employee engagement would be a worthwhile investment. If employees are at their place of work for any reason other than sharing their talents, skills, and knowledge in work they truly enjoy, they will not be partners in the process.

Positive psychologists remind us that employees who are valued and respected, allowed to use their talents and abilities to the fullest, seen as partners in productivity achievements, rewarded for their optimism and creativity, and feel as if they can be authentically themselves will devote themselves to their work and drive themselves to unbelievable excellence.[9]

Unfortunately, there seems to be a pervading belief—one that originated in the early 1920's—that in order to motivate employees and keep them engaged, there must be plenty of extrinsic incentives. This worn-out perspective continues to proclaim that if employees are not compensated adequately using extrinsic reward systems, they will be lazy, unmotivated, and habitually disengaged. This view also touts that all that's expected of employees is that they just need to show up, do their job, and obey management. According to this out-dated motivational strategy, by using extrinsic motivation as a carrot, managers can expect exemplary performance. Sound familiar?

As I've indicated before, extrinsic employee engagement (*e*-engagement) strategies are not the elixir they used to be. They may make it more difficult for top performers to shop around for higher stimulus employment; however, as soon as they can find similar *e*-perks somewhere else, they will leave the nest! And in many cases they will leave knowing there may be less *e*-perks waiting for them. Why? Because people:

- value being respected,
- want meaningful work,
- need opportunities to be creative,
- want to contribute to something they feel is significant and worthwhile,
- want to be genuinely listened to,
- need to have their ideas valued and used,
- value being able to pursue personal growth interests,

- enjoy working in environments compatible with their own beliefs and values, and
- want to feel they are part of a 'community' that has a heart.

Believe it or not, they want these things as much as, and often even more than money!

These views on employee engagement are substaniated by the current research. The *e*-perks that characterize e-engagement strategies are simply temporary engagement drivers. Of course I advocate their continued use, but not their 'pedestalled status.' I categorically recommend *i*-engagement (intrinsic) strategies for sustainable and enduring employee engagement. It's important to recognize that it has always been the intrinsic motivators (*i*-motivators) more than the extrinsic drivers (*e*-drivers) that have interested employees the most.

What's required now is what's always been required. It's called "sustainable engagement." The key factor, studies find, is a work environment that more fully energizes employees by promoting their physical, emotional, and social well-being. Add to that mental and spiritual well being—or more specifically, the increased energy derived from the capacity for true immersion in their work and a strong sense of purpose.

Many employers are pursuing a variety of wellness efforts, typically focused on giving thoughtful incentives and rewards to people who embrace healthy behaviors like exercise, good diet or effective management of a chronic illness, the report concludes.

These are important, but to sustain energy, employers have to go beyond these core programs and embrace the notion of workplace energy on a far broader plane. When they do, the consequences are nothing short of staggering. For organizations in general, and leaders specifically, the challenge is to shift from their traditional focus on getting more out of people, to investing in meeting people's core needs so they're freed, fueled, and inspired to bring more of themselves to work. [10]

This *Extraordinary Leadership* book was developed in response to the rising voices of those researchers, scientists, and pragmatic organizational development consultants who are serious about guaranteeing sustainable, enduring, and practical employee engagement that uses both *i*-drivers and *e*-drivers to foster it.

While organizations need both intrinsic and extrinsic employee engagement strategies, there must be just as great, if not more, of an emphasis on i-drivers to make the employee engagement formula complete—and realistic.

This approach is visionary, but pragmatic; forward-thinking, yet present moment focused; strategic, yet tactical; founded on scientific principles, but proven to work outside the lab.

You will find the Extraordinary Leadership approach exactly what you've been looking for because it places just as much responsibility and accountability for exemplary engagement on your direct reports as it does on you. Employee engagement is a partnership, not an entitlement program. And it starts with your ability to make the connection with your Extraordinary Nature!

I'm not going to kid you. Establishing a conscious connection with your "Extraordinary You" isn't for the faint of heart. Why? Because it will take you, as a leader, having more willpower than won't power. It means being willing to discover the Real You. It asks you to believe in current research and apply it to yourself, your employees, and your work environment. It takes courage and patience. It demands commitment to being the best you can be—so your employees can be the best they can be. It requires disciplined effort and a belief in yourself.

Will it be worth it? You betcha! Will you be glad you stayed the course? Absolutely! Will you be seen as an Extraordinary Leader? Without one iota of a doubt! I have interviewed enough leaders, studied enough research, and know positively from my

Introduction

own professional experience that discovering your Core Nature is the Holy Grail of the leadership experience! It is priceless and monumentally fulfilling! It's like hitting the 'leadership lottery.'

Spend some quality time with this book yourself before you share the concepts with your employees. Uncover the 'Real You.' Discover what an Extraordinary Leader ... what an extraordinary person ... you are. Begin to see the extraordinariness in others too ... and draw it out of them.

Let me know how you're doing. I'd love to get an email, text, or tweet that says, *"I've truly become one with my Extraordinary Nature and I'm having the most fulfilling leadership experience ever! I'm also helping my employees find their Extraordinary Nature. And I'm happy to report that employee engagement is at an all time high!"*

Chapter 1: Authentegrity

The privilege of a lifetime is to become who you truly are." (C.G. Jung)

Authentegrity is one of the most essential Core Abilities, especially for leaders, so that's why it's the first one on the list. Okay—I think I made the word "Authentegrity" up! It is a combination of two valuable qualities: Authenticity and Integrity. And if it is consistently expressed in the way you manage people, it can lead to unlimited commitment, engagement, teamwork, and exceptional customer experiences—all of which open the way to the very highest possibilities for productivity and professional success. Michael Kernis and Brian Goldman defined authenticity as "the unimpeded operation of one's true or core self in one's daily enterprise.[1] It relates to how we encounter external forces, pressures, and influences presented to us by the external world. Combine this with the meaning of integrity as defined by Alan Cohen who explained that "You are in integrity when the life you are living on the outside matches who you are on the inside"—and you have defined the Core Ability of Authentegrity. Authentegrity is the degree to which we are true to our own spirit, values, core beliefs, and character, despite external pressures and organization demands.

Here's a secret that can really help all leaders: People want to be led by someone "real." Leadership demands the expression of an authentic self. Try to lead like someone else, and you will fail. Employees will not follow leaders who invest little of themselves in their leadership behaviors. This is partly a reaction to the turbulent times we live in. It is also a response to the public's widespread disenchantment with politicians and businesspeople. We all suspect that we're being duped. Our growing dissatisfaction with sleek, artificial, airbrushed leadership is what makes Authentegrity such a desirable quality in today's business world—a quality that, unfortunately, is in short supply. Leaders and followers both associate Authentegrity with sincerity, honesty, and integrity. It's the real thing—the attribute that uniquely defines great leaders.[2]

Once you achieve that internal connection, you can be more harmonious with life around you, and more confident in your ability to lead. The question is, how can you live in that higher state of awareness that allows you to be more connected mentally, emotionally, and physically? The answer is that the more you live in the deeper parts of your being, rather than the superficial parts of your ego's wants and desires, the greater will be the affinity, connection, and harmony within you, and with your surroundings, including the people within your sphere of influence.

It's important to understand what guides you throughout your life — discover your signature strengths, and the basis of your true stature. Then you can intentionally apply those signature strengths in your everyday living. That means having the courage to acknowledge your limitations and embrace your vulnerabilities. It demands working toward integration, alignment, and the congruence of your ordinary self with your Extraordinary Nature.

What Does Science Say?

In a ground-breaking study that remains the largest in-depth study of leaders based on first-person interviews, Bil George determined that authentic leaders are constantly growing and learning from their leadership experiences. They are able to reflect on past experiences and apply what they have learned to new challlenges they face ... and they are able to learn from other leaders.[3] Multiple studies reveal that leaders with a high degree of Authentegrity respond to their intrinsic motives rather than being influenced by power, money, recognition, or expediency. They exercise autonomy. They dismiss the illusions of outer appearances. They make a conscious effort to choose among the extrinsic motives available to them. Their thoughts, beliefs, words, and actions originate deep from within and they are secure enough in their own integrity to resist self-defeating and destructive external pressures.

Accoring to researcher Laura Kinsler, authentic leaders with integrity embody both self-awareness and self-regulation. Their leadership reflects:
- objective decision-making;
- the ability to act honestly and openly;
- the courage to act in line with one's own beliefs and values;
- a sense of ethics and moral values;
- an invested interest in development and scces of others.[4]

In short, the path they choose is congruent with their Authentic Self —their Authentegrity.

On the other hand, actions misaligned with our Authentic Self are alien, false, fake, pretentious, stressful, insincere, fraudulent, strained, bogus, and phony—to say the least. This is typical of leaders who are off balance, indecisive, chronically stressed, alienated, detached, and, well, just plain difficult to work with.

Of course, everyone wants to claim they are operating from Authentegrity! The problem is that anyone can make that claim and reap the benefits of what the word implies. I hear concepts like transparency, genuineness, trust, support, and open communication tossed around the workplace all the time. That's good, right? Well, it depends. Like the duckling that appears to glide across the water, there can be turbulence beneath the surface. If you pay attention, you'll notice quite a few people who want to stir up trouble while invoking the halo-effect associated with the words implying Authentegrity. As with the duckling, what's on the surface can be deceiving. So, which is authentic? What's on the surface or what's underneath?[5]

Leaders who are aligned with their Extraordinary Nature act with more interest, purposefulness, excitement, and confidence, often demonstrating superior performance, persistence, creativity, vitality, self-esteem, and general well-being than those who operate from deceptive or power-driven motives. Their employees tend to be more engaged, creative, and driven to perform than those who work for inauthentic leaders.

Here's an Example of Authentegrity:

It's all about Rule 13-4c, which is professional golf's peculiar policy that prohibits a player from touching any loose impediment in a hazard—even a single leaf—as part of the maneuver to dislodge the ball. Golf's rules only allow for two options – certainty or, if a golfer isn't sure whether he/she broke a rule, then he/she is presumed guilty of breaking that rule.

In late October, 2012, Golfer Blayne Barber was unsure if his club had brushed a leaf in the bunker on the 13th hole at Callaway Gardens. His caddy was certain it had not moved. Barber went on to play based on his caddie's insistence that he had not moved the leaf. But three days later, the incident was still weighing heavily on his mind. He was just unsure about whether or not he had actually moved the leaf.

On November 2, six days after the tournament ended, Barber called the PGA to report his situation. Because he had signed an incorrect scorecard, he was disquallified. His decision potentially could cost him the opportunity of competing for millions of dollars. But Barber said there are some things more important than money. When interviewed, he said, "I don't know why all this is happening. I don't know what it will entail in the future, but maybe it will have an effect on someone, maybe someone will learn from it. It's a lot bigger than me. I just wanted to do my part to make it right and clear my conscience.

"I just feel peace about it," Barber adds. "Doing the right thing and doing what I know is right in my heart and in my conscience is more important than short-term success."

If you've ever met a leader with a high degree of Authentegrity, I think you'll agree that there's something very special about him or her. Authentic leaders are like magnets. They attract your attention. They have woven their scattered parts into a solid, coherent, integrated whole. Their thoughts, actions, and emotions stem from their essence, rather than old patterns, antiquated assumptions, and worn-out beliefs. They have a clear sense of what doesn't match with who they really are.

I'd like to pause for a moment to talk about the type of work you find yourself in. It's possible you aren't doing what you'd like to be doing. But just because you are doing work you are not completely passionate about does not mean you are out of integrity. It might be that you have found yourself in a position where you need a certain income or benefits to sustain your lifestyle. Doing work that creates stability in your life could be a way of working within your Authentegrity Core Ability.

The ultimate issue is *how* you are doing whatever work you do! If you are working in a job that forces you to consistently and regularly operate in conflict with your Authentegrity, red flag warnings should be popping up all around you! No amount of money or power is worth the sacrifice of your Authentegrity!

If you're not where you want to be in the work that you're doing, it might be because you are unweaving old belief structures, and this takes ongoing, persistent, and patient action. Take a good look at how your current work is serving the Authentic You and take the necessary actions to align your work with your Core Nature. Barbara de Angelis, relationship consultant, agrees. She says, "We need to find the courage to say NO to the things and people that are not serving us if we want to rediscover ourselves and live our lives with authenticity."

However, that does not mean that you should make hasty decisions— nor should you procrastinate. Take the right actions that make sense for you in this moment—NOW—to square yourself with the Extraordinary You.

It may mean staying right where you are and looking at your current work differently, or it may mean finding your true work somewhere else. Whichever route you decide to take, make sure you can say, "I am absolutely clear that this is what I must do." Sometimes it takes these moments of clarity to shift gears and embrace who you are rather than trying to be someone you're not.

There's no denying that we are being pulled in many different directions these days. Oftentimes it's difficult for us to feel we can be effective, successful, and emotionally satisfied all of the time. Whether in business or in our personal lives, if seeking out our Authentic Self leads us to be more in tune with our core needs and more comfortable in our own skin, it's a journey worth taking.

> When you're authentic, you're true to yourself. When your brand is authentic, it is true to its mission and purpose. The power in authenticity, whether in your brand or person, is that it leaves no questions unanswered. People know where you stand, what you're made of and what is important to you. Authenticity helps you define how they see you, without risking they'll be confused.
>
> When you're wishy-washy, there's a lack of definition. Thus, there's a lack of authenticity. When you contradict yourself, there's lack of definition. Thus, there's a lack of authenticity. When you always agree, follow the crowd and never stand for something on your own, there's a lack of definition. Thus, there's a lack of authenticity.
>
> Being authentic means you know who you are. You define your place and parcel in life. You stand for something. And by being true to that something, no one ever questions the truth about you.[6]
>
> (J. Falls)

Authentegrity Versus Differentiation

Executives ask one question on an almost weekly basis: "How can I differentiate my company in the marketplace?" Sohrab Vossoughi shared what he believed to be the only reply to every president, chief executive officer, or vice-president of marketing: "*Why* do you want to be different?" He went on to share a very interesting (and somewhat contrarian) viewpoint:

> We are swimming in an overabundance of products and services. Different is no longer a differentiator. What is? Creating an authentic relationship with your customers. Authenticity in business is a distinctly 21st century concept made relevant by a confluence of factors. The public's trust of businesses and institutions is in steep decline. Consumers' media savvy has pulled back the wizard's curtain on insincere marketing ploys that are only surface-sexy. Reality TV and online personae and avatars have redefined our sense of reality, bringing the question of what is real into mainstream dialogue. Consumers seek meaning and a brand they can trust. They are busy creating ways to cut through the noise in search of products and services that resonate with integrity and transparency; in a word, authenticity *(I would change that word to Authentegrity)*. That quest for authenticity is a call to action for any company intending to be relevant in the 21st century.[7]

When you begin to awaken to your Authentic Self, the same 'Self' neuroscientists call your "Deeper Self," you discover that being fully alive and aware are suddenly recognized to be deep and profoundly creative experiences. You begin to appreciate the barest murmurings of your own struggle to become fully conscious of your incredible uniqueness and extraordinariness.

The alignment process—calibrating your ordinary self with your fine-tuned Deeper Self—is an experiential process. It demands our inner resolve and undivided loyalty. You cannot serve two masters, as the saying goes. Author Sidney Sheldon strived very hard to be real by refusing to be tempted to 'serve two masters.' He asserted, "Believable action is based on authenticity, and accuracy is very important to me. I always spend time researching my novels, exploring the customs and attitudes of the country I'm using for their setting." Anyone who's read his novels can attest to the authentegrity in his writings.

Most of the outer labels that define you place you in boxes or categories relative to other people. You probably join the majority of people who identify themselves by race, gender, religion, political views, occupation, and so on. Many of those labels were given to us by birth or awarded to us by circumstance; and all of them inform our point of view about ourselves and the world we live in. But none of them are who we really are. They are not our Core Essence. They are simply socialized labels that put us into convenient boxes that can be managed, directed, and controlled.

One thing is for sure, the more you live on the surface of who you really are, the less you are in touch with your Extraordinary Nature. The problem is that the more you look outside of yourself to create a sense of your True Self, the farther off track you get. How can you know who you truly are when you spend your time and attention trying to be something you're not?

No amount of counterfeiting yourself to gain the approval of others is going to bring you any closer to really knowing yourself. Living from a place of profound Authentegrity involves being rooted in your deepest beliefs, values, truths, and principles—and living a life that is a true reflection of those core essences. Each day becomes a self-editing process where you do more and more of those things that are in alignment with the Extraordinary You and less and less of those things which aren't a reflection of who you really are. This is, indeed, the very essence of being an Extraordinary Leader.

Strengthening Your Authentegrity

Here are some things you can do to strengthen your Core Ability of Authentegrity, to be an Extraordinary Leader:

1. **Give up perfectionism.** Leaders who believe they need to be perfect never reveal their true selves to their people. As a result, their people feel uncomfortable admitting they need help or sharing problems they are experiencing. The workplace becomes a masquerade where everyone projects they know it all, and productivity suffers. Be vulnerable. Admit what you don't know. Let your employees be the heroes as they share their knowledge.

2. **Admit mistakes and take responsibility for your decisions and actions.** This goes hand-in-hand with giving up perfectionism, because it asks you to acknowledge when you are wrong. Nothing brings people to your corner more than when you show you are willing to admit you are wrong. By focusing on how to fix it, you model behavior you want to see among your employees.

3. **Be as transparent as possible while maintaining necessary confidentiality.** This is a difficult tightrope walk for leaders, but one that is vital to your crediblity. Share information as openly as you can, because people cannot be empowered unless they have the information they need to make wise decisions. However, there are some things that cannot be shared, and it is perfectly acceptable for you, as an Extraordinary Leader, to simply let your folks know this is the case. This way, they can work with confidence, and believe the things you tell them.

4. **Welcome contrarian opinions.** Truly authentic leaders know the value of gathering different points of view, and know how to generate them without creating unhealthy conflict.

5. **Don't hesitate to make the right business decision, even when that choice may cost money.** Leaders operating out of Authentegrity realize that every business decision has an opportunity cost. They know that opportunity costs always include the cost of the second-best choice. For example, if they decide to spend money on the research and development team, it could mean their organization forgoes the chance to allocate money to an interest-bearing investment fund. The opportunity cost in this case is the amount of money their organization would otherwise have earned in the investment account.

   Authentic leaders also know they must make choices related to non-cash assets, such as time and labor. For instance, the choice to have IT staff upgrade the firm's customer database may create an opportunity cost of upgrading the firm's accounting database. Coming from a place of Authentegrity requires a leader to consider both the seen and unseen costs associated with decisions, and be willing to do what is right ... even when it costs money, time, energy, and effort.

   All of this being said, authentic leaders seldom, if ever, succumb to what is called 'the sunk-cost fallacy' (throwing good money after bad). They know when to say when, and pull the plug on projcts that are not producing the results expected.

6. **Be "fully present" when talking with others.** If you are busy planning what you are going to say when it's your turn to talk, there is no way you can really hear what the other person is saying. Nothing demonstrates Authentegrity more than paying attention.

7. **Know your values, and walk your talk.** Why is it important to understand what you value most? Because when you know what you value, you can make decisions and lead others from a place of alignment and truth. Here's a quick personal values assessment to get you started:

Values Clarification

Identify a maximum of 10 values that are extremely important to you by placing a check mark beside them.

- ☐ Achievement/Accomplishing goals
- ☐ Advancement/Moving up in chosen field
- ☐ Affiliation/Sense of belonging
- ☐ Authenticity/Matching actions with values & beliefs
- ☐ Being Responsible for my thoughts, words, & actions
- ☐ Competitiveness /Feeling a sense of being the best
- ☐ Creativity/Being imaginative/Questioning unquestioned answers
- ☐ Daily self-care practices (i.e., yoga, meditation, exercise)
- ☐ Family/Relationship & time with loved ones
- ☐ Friendships/Relationships outside of family
- ☐ Giving Consciousness/Generosity
- ☐ Health & Well-being
- ☐ Helping Others/Compassion/Service/Social action
- ☐ Independence/Autonomy
- ☐ Inner Harmony
- ☐ Integrity/Honesty/Trustworthiness
- ☐ Keeping Commitments
- ☐ Leisure Time/Hobbies & interests, rest & relaxation)
- ☐ Order/Structure
- ☐ Personal Development
- ☐ Power
- ☐ Recognition
- ☐ Respect
- ☐ Responsibility
- ☐ Risk-Taking
- ☐ Sense of Humor
- ☐ Spiritual Growth
- ☐ Spiritual or Religious Affiliations
- ☐ Teamwork
- ☐ Thirst for Knowledge
- ☐ Truth
- ☐ Wealth

Step 2: Narrow your list to five values. (I know ... this is really tough! But take a few minutes to think about all the items you checked, and come up with the five that mean the most to you.)

Step 3: Prioritize these five values. Now it gets really tough. Here is one way to do it. List each of your five values on a separate notecard. Line them up in front of you so you can look at all five at the same time. Now, imagine that you can achieve the most important goal of your life. All you have to do is give up one value. Choose which one and set it aside, face-up.

As you look at the four remaining values, imagine you can help your company meet their most critical objective to be outrageously profitable. All you have to do is give up one value. Choose which one, and set it aside, face-up, on top of the one you already set aside.

Next, as you look at the three remaining values, imagine you could solve world hunger forever. No child would ever go hungry again. All you have to do is give up one value. Choose which one, and set it aside, face-up, on top of the ones you already set aside.

Finally, as you look at the two remaining values, imagine you have the power to bring about world peace. No more war! All you have to do is ... you guessed it ... give up one value. Decide which one of the remaining values you will give up, and set it aside, face-up, on top of the ones you already set aside.

You are left with one value. This is your most important value. Set it on top of the others, and you now have your top five values, in prioritized order. List them here. You'll be using them later.

#1: _____

#2: _____

#3: _____

#4: _____

#5: _____

The Ability & the Color: Summary

Authentegrity: Aligning your thoughts, words, and actions with the authentic values you embrace. Being true, genuine, and real — no matter what the situation or results. Doing what you say you'll do.

The Color Red: Red is the color of energy and passion. It signifies your life force, and represents determination and conviction. Red is the color of Authentegrity because when you operate from that place of alignment, you live from conviction and intention, and are able to embrace life with energy and passion, knowing you are being true to the Extraordinary You!

Using the Color Red:

If you want to strengthen your awareness of your Authentegrity, make red your color of focus. Choose to wear something red as part of your wardrobe; eat foods that are red in color (apples, cherries, kidney beans, tomatoes, strawberries, red peppers, salsa, red-velvet cake, etc.); place items that are red in your environment (red flowers, a red stone, pictures with red as a dominant color); use red ink or markers when you write.

While this may feel a little silly at first, allow yourself to give it a try without judgment. Become aware of how much stronger you feel in terms of living in alignment with your values, and how you are experiencing Authentegrity in your life.

Cultivating Your Authentegrity

All I would tell people is to hold on to what was individual about themselves, not to allow their ambition for success to cause them to try to imitate the success of others. You've got to find it on your own terms.
(Harrison Ford)

Laser Focus Technique:

Preparation:

Prepare for this Laser Focus experience by finding a quiet location where you will be uninterrupted. Sit in a comfortable position that you can hold for 20-25 minutes.

Take a few deep breaths, exhaling slowly between each breath. Without trying to force your breath in any way, allow it to find its own natural depth and rhythm. Always breathe through your nose (That's assuming your nasal passages are clear and unobstructed. Otherwise breathe through your mouth.)

Allow your attention to focus either on the sensation of your breath coming and going through your nostrils, or on the rising and falling of your belly as you breathe.

Give your full attention to the coming and going of your breath.

If you realize your attention has wandered, and you find yourself engrossed in thinking ahead or day-dreaming, simply acknowledge the ego's trespass, then gently but firmly bring your attention back to your breathing.

The Process:

In your mind's eye, focus on the word " authentegrity." Say the word "authentegrity" to yourself. Repeat it silently when you inhale and repeat it again when you exhale. Do this five times in succession each time you inhale and exhale.

Now, this time, when you inhale repeat the word "authentegrity" silently as you did before. However, when you exhale, say the word "authentegrity" aloud. Do this for the next series of five breaths.

Focus on your breathing, paying attention to the rise and fall of your abdomen, without thinking or saying a word.

The next time you inhale, think silently, "I am." When you exhale think, "in complete authentegrity." When you inhale again think, "with my Core Essence." When you exhale, do not think or say anything. Do all of this by breathing normally.

Repeat this "I am – in complete authentegrity – with my Core Essence" sequence of breaths five times, breathing normally as you do so.

Focus once again on your breathing, paying attention to the rise and fall of your abdomen, without thinking or saying a word.

Now, think of a situation (present or future) in your personal or professional life where you can use your Authentegrity to achieve a positive outcome. See yourself as the epitome of a competent, confident, compassionate harmonizing influence. Take whatever time you need to mentally orchestrate your ability to create an authentic, integrity-driven outcome.

See yourself being sensitive to another person's needs, showing compassion, being diplomatic and tactful, communicating clearly, demonstrating objectivity and common sense, being patient and thoughtful, showing respect and reasonableness.

Take as long as you need to satisfy yourself that you have shown that you can be an authentically positive influence.

Use the sequence of "I am – in complete authentegrity – with my Core Essence" breaths again, repeating the sequence three times.

I invite you to use this "Authentegrity Laser Focus Technique" as an equilibrium-establishing safety valve before you enter into an emotion-packed experience, one where you suspect emotions will run high. Once you anticipate what might happen and see yourself exhibiting Authentegrity, you will increase the chances of achieving the outcome you desire. (By the way, this is the same mental process world class athletes use to prepare for their competitions).

The more you see yourself as centered and balanced, the greater your connection will be with the Extraordinary You.

Self-Directed Activity to Develop Your Authentegrity Core Ability: Star Player

This activity revisits and deepens your Values Clarification exercise, helping you strengthen your ability to operate from a place of Authentegrity regardless of the situation. By practicing small acts of Authentegrity and reinforcing them, you are able to call upon this Core Ability in difficult moments that result in life-changing consequences.

Part 1: Revisit the Values Clarification exercise you took earlier in this chapter. List your prioritized top five values which you have identified as the foundations for your life.

1. _____
2. _____
3. _____
4. _____
5. _____

Take some quality time to reflect on these five values, to be sure they resonate with who you are at your deepest core. Define each one as it relates to the way you use them as your "North Star" in decision-making and living. Be sure you have a very clear understanding of each value, and what it means to you. Once you do this, you are ready to move on to Part 2 of this Self-Directed Activity.

Part 2: Draw a big 5-pointed star (or use the one pictured here). At each point, write one of your values. Once you have completed these first two steps, you will be able to revisit this activity often, using your star's power to jump right into Part 3.

Part 3: Reflect back on your past few days of work. Identify a situation or interaction that jumps out at you. It can be a positive one, or one that left you feeling frustrated, uncomfortable, or stressful. Recall how you responded or reacted in the situation, then determine which of your 5 values came into play. Ask yourself these questions:

- Did I respond with intention, or simply react to the situation?

- How did this situation or interaction make me feel? How did it make the others involved in the situation feel?

- Did I choose to respond or react from one of my core values, or did I sacrifice a value?

- If I acted from Authentegrity, what was the payoff for me? What was the cost?

- If I sacrificed a value, what was the pay-off for me? Was it worth it?

- How intentional were my thoughts, choices, and actions as they related to my five Core Values?

- What outside influences affected the way I handled this situation, and how much power did I give those influences versus my values?

- What can I learn from this to help me operate from my highest level of Authentegrity in the future?

Personal Reflections

*Date:*_____

Chapter 2
Intuitive Wisdom

It requires wisdom to understand wisdom; the music is nothing if the audience is deaf. (Walter Lippmann)

As a leader, have you ever done something that had a negative consequence, and immediately thought, "I knew I shouldn't have done that!" Or perhaps you had a feeling you should take some action, even though it made no practical sense—and the result was something powerful. What you instinctively knew came from your Core Ability of Intuitive Wisdom. We all have that incredible ability within us, which we call on for inner guidance and discernment. As we strengthen our Core Ability of Intuitive Wisdom, we are able to make decisions and take actions based on "uncommon sense." We trust that sixth sense of intuition and move forward regardless of what outer appearances may indicate. It's more than just what we know intellectually. There's a difference between knowledge and wisdom. For example, one could say that knowledge is the awareness that a tomato is a fruit; intuitive wisdom is knowing NOT to use it in a fruit salad!

Let's look at a couple of very simple leadership examples in everyday life. Have you ever gathered your team, preparing to have lunch together, and you pose the question to the team, "Where do you want to go to eat?" It can become very frustrating when everyone responds with, "Oh, I don't care. Whatever everyone else wants to do is fine with me." It can lead to a long decision-making period, and a short lunch time! This is a common and basic example of not allowing our Intuitive Wisdom to emerge!

Or how about dealing with one of your employees who is difficult to get along with? Have you ever just known the right thing to say to manage the relationship, even when others couldn't? Or maybe you have been working on a project at work and run into a roadblock of some kind. Even though you'd never experienced this particular type of problem before, you discovered a way to work around it and achieve a positive result.

Even with such simple situations as these, we can call on our Intuitive Wisdom, which is the Core Ability to apply what we know, and discern the right thing to do. We're talking about more than book learning. Intuitive Wisdom is a deep inner knowing that goes beyond the known facts. In fact (to play on words), sometimes the things we think we already know can interfere with our deeper Intuitive Wisdom.

How many times has someone said, "Let's look at the facts." It sounds so simple. But wait ... what, exactly, are the facts? How do we know "truth" when we hear it? It's not always as simple as it seems.

About the "Facts..."

From reading this book, you can tell that it is deeply immersed in the research related to neuroscience, positive psychology, and other sciences. But even research can become confusing. For example, you would think research would confirm what is true. But I found clear, well-documented research that reported five cups of coffee a day may cut heart disease—and another equally well-documented study that indicated drinking five or more cups of coffee a day increases the risk of having heart problems! One study claimed coffee is good for you because it helps prevent Parkinson's and diabetes, while another said coffee is bad for you because it contributes to osteoporosis. What's a coffee lover to do? Choose the research that supports what you want to do, of course!

This happens with leadership strategies on a regular basis! There are many leaders who support every "Flavor of the Month" that comes down the pike, automatically believing the marketing around it—even when the research is faulty or doesn't even relate to the technique at all! For example, they see an image of a group of people celebrating success, tied to an article supporting the benefits of self-directed work teams. Without even evaluating the authenticity of the article, they make the connection in their heads and sign up! Then it becomes "The Emperor's Clothes" syndrome.

You may recall the story by Hans Christian Anderson, about an egotistical emperor who commissioned two weavers to create a suit of clothes that was invisible to anyone unfit or incompetent for their position, or just plain stupid. The weavers, of course, were swindlers who realized no one would admit they could not see the fabric. Everyone claimed it was the most amazing fabric ever seen! The emperor could not see the fabric (since it did not really exist), but he did not want to appear unfit for his position! So he allowed himself to be "dressed" in it and paraded down the street to show it off! Everyone claimed how incredible the emperor's new clothes were (not wanting to admit they could not see anything!) Finally a small child exclaimed, "But he doesn't have anything on! The emperor isn't wearing any clothes!" And everyone suddenly realized they'd been duped!

This is exactly what happens with "Flavor of the Month" leadership strategies. Once people invest in them, they are hesitant to say they did not work. After all, they don't want to admit they made a bad investment. Before long, others have adopted the strategies based on the false testimonials, and then everyone wants to do it! And then some contrarian leader, researcher, or consultant speaks out and verifies it doesn't work—and everyone breathes a sigh of relief that they no longer need to keep up the charade. Sound familiar? Innate Wisdom was definitely on vacation.

Then there's the issue of "Leadership Junk-o-logic!" Junk-o-logic began as a 1950s advertising principle (still alive and well) that says you can give someone any two unrelated ideas and act like they're related, and that person will make up a connection. Open a magazine, look at a billboard, or stop fast forwarding through TV commercials for a few minutes, and chances are you'll be seeing an image that has nothing to do with the product (for example, dogs and pharmeceuticals). Advertisers are hoping your Intuitive Wisdom is in the OFF mode as you watch their commercials!

And then, there are the truths that really *are* proven, but still seem so farfetched that we wonder—who cares? For example, did you know it is true that a duck's quack does not echo? Would you believe research has proven there are more plastic flamingos in the U.S. than real ones? And how about this? In 1939, Ernest Vincent Wright wrote a novel, *Gadsby* (not to be confused with the classic by F. Scott Fitzgerald, *The Great Gatsby*), which contains over 50,000 words—none of which contain the letter E! A few more truths for you to ponder: The electric chair was invented by a dentist (totally believable)! If you yelled for 8 years, 7 months and 6 days, you would have produced enough sound energy to heat one cup of coffee (which may or may not be good for you, depending on which research you believe)!

Okay, by now you are probably asking, so what's the point? What does this have to do with leadership? Here's the deal: Whether we are talking about research, personal opinions, politics, lifestyles, or leadership in the workplace, the bottom line is the same: When we hear conflicting information, we must use our Intuitive Wisdom to discern the truth and value of that information ... and make the appropriate choices and decisions.

That's what this Core Ability is all about! Through this Core Ability, we are able to move beyond raw emotions or different opinions, and make sound judgments about how we handle situations. We are able to make the appropriate choice even when there is a part of us that wants to do something different. With Intuitive Wisdom, we know the difference between worrying about a situation versus taking actions that bring solutions. With Intuitive Wisdom, we know the difference between playing the victim card, versus standing firm in our authenticity and integrity. We can discern the difference between the short-lived satisfaction of revenge and the long-term peacefulness of forgiveness. With Intuitive Wisdom, we make the choice to practice Extraordinary Leadership with every word, decision, and action we make.

What Does Science Say?

It's not just me championing the Core Ability of Intuitive Wisdom. Research from Harvard Graduate School of Education has proven that this Core Ability helps you:

- stay calm and centered;
- better manage uncomfortable feelings and difficult interactions;
- think more clearly and compassionately;
- discern where to direct your time and energy;
- sustain your enthusiasm; and
- achieve results.

These discernments will help you make wise decisions and savor the joy of leadership. Through guided mindfulness practices and exercises, inner focus techniques, case studies, reflection, presentations, growth scenarios, and large and small group discussion, you will become more discerning and able to renew your commitment to action, guided by the values that inspire you to make a difference.

Sound judgment helps you identify common patterns of overreaction, and then learn how to respond to difficulties with awareness, poise, and resilience. It helps you respond deliberately rather than react automatically, to be guided by your values rather than be derailed by your discomfort. It helps you explore skills for self-awareness and self-renewal so you can sustain your leadership and service to others with insight, wisdom, and warmth—and renew your incredible capacity for wise appraisal.[1]

Becoming a wiser leader goes beyond book learning. It is an exercise in intentional inner development. Like any skill you want to develop, it takes discipline and effort. A good starting point for advanced inner work is to turn to wisdom writings and philosophies that discuss the further reaches of human development.

Such writings, in turn, will lead you to do-it-yourself activities such as focused awareness practices, self-knowledge strategies, ego-transcending opportunities, and oneness-realization. Reading about these things is not a substitute for the practices themselves, but reading can help you understand them, introduce new ideas and activities, and perhaps motivate you to try them.

Novels, biographies, and autobiographies are valuable resources for the development of practical wisdom because they are filled with examples of wise and unwise behavior, skillful and unskillful handling of life situations. As you read them you may want to ask yourself questions like: How does their thinking, choices, and behavior differ from 'ordinary' people? What values and core beliefs guide their lives? What perspectives and interpretations of life situations do they use to guide their actions?

For those who want to develop existential, ontological, spiritual wisdom, the world's philosophical and spiritual literature are vital intellectual resources. In addition, reading the latest scientific research and discoveries would be a 'wise' thing to do to gain a pragmatic perspective about the world we live in and how things work. Readings in the neurosciences, positive psychology, genetics, biology, sociology, and quantum physics will add tremendous depth to your intuitive wisdom.

But reading is not enough! Inner Wisdom is strengthened through use. Life itself instructs us. Experiencing a multitude of varied life experiences can teach us much about ourselves ... and about Extraordinary Leadership.

As an Extraordinary Leader, it is important to recognize the areas you are involved in that could be enhanced by using your Core Ability of Intuitive Wisdom. Whenever you realize you are vacillating between options, or struggling to handle a situation, or regretting your behavior, that's the time to stop—immediately—and call on your Core Ability of Intuitive Wisdom to help you.

Structuring our lives so that we have many kinds of experiences helps us keep an open, curious, inquisitive, appreciative mental perspective so that we get the most out of whatever experiences we have. Travel is a great eye-opener. It helps us get to know people with different skills, outlooks, and values. Wisdom develops when people go through the key "learning-from-life" process, where they reflect, integrate, and apply the lessons that they have learned, in and out of class, on and off campus, to their lives. The three conditions that directly facilitate the development of Intuitive Wisdom are a person's orientation to:

- learning,
- life experiences, and
- interactions with others.

> **Putting It Into Practice:**
>
> Reflect on your experiences over the past few weeks at work. What kinds of situations have you been involved in that could have been improved with a healthy dose of Intuitive Wisdom?
>
> Now think about situations where you paid attention to your Intuitive Wisdom and handled things with poise, confidence, and effectiveness.
>
> What was the difference?

These conditions all take place in a particular environment, with a context that influences a person's orientation to learning and development.[2] Engaging in different kinds of work experiences broadens your perspectives as a leader. Taking up a variety of hobbies enriches your life too, and can take you further down the path toward uncommon wisdom.

> Wisdom involves seeing things as they are, seeing the essence not through the frame of reference; seeing and understanding deeply human situations; knowing when and where to act and where not to act; perfect adjustment to the situation; ability to see and foresee different problems and avoid them.[3]
>
> (S. M. Cohen)

Hanging out with people who are already living the beliefs and values you'd like to make your own can be most helpful as you seek to deepen your Wise Self. Make a practice to watch YouTubes, videos, and DVD's of wise people. In addition, Facebooking, tweeting, emailing, writing, and meeting with people you consider intuitively wise can be on-going sources of guidance and growth.

Pay attention to your own experiences, so you can learn to recognize your inner wisdom when it speaks to you. When you get that "I knew I should have..." feeling, take a moment and recall what the feeling you ignored felt like. This way, you reinforce what it is so you can follow that guidance next time.

Perhaps a quote by Albert Einstein can best describe the power of developing our Intuitive Wisdom. It involves the intentional process of developing the inner knowing that is at the center of our being. Here's what Einstein says:

> *The most beautiful and profound emotion we can experience is the sensation of the mystical. It is the power of all true sciences. He to whom this emotion is a stranger, who can no longer wonder and stand rapt in awe, is as good as dead. To know what is impenetrable to us really exists, manifesting itself as the highest wisdom and the most radiant beauty which our dull faculties can comprehend only in the most primitive form—this knowledge, this feeling is at the center of our true being.*

The 'true being' he is referring to is the Extraordinary You, the Core Essence of you, the One-of-a-kind-You—the YOU who possesses the highest wisdom and inner knowing. Too often we are encouraged to seek answers to questions outside ourselves rather than explore our own inner wisdom. We are taught to find the expert, read a book, seek advice. But our journey is one of opening from the inside out, learning to look for answers, to go deep into our hearts and souls where we can connect with the inner wisdom and receive guidance from within to transform our lives.

> **Putting It Into Practice:**
> What books have you read that made an impact on you — and how did you change as a result?
>
> What personal experiences/interests have you had that helped you grow as a leader?
>
> What experiences in the work setting have had a positive effect on you—and what did you learn? What have you learned from difficult experiences?
>
> Who among your acquaintances would you consider to be "wise?" What is it that creates that perception? How have these people changed you?

Two major research groups stand out as valuable contributors to the scientific study of wisdom: Paul Baltes and his colleagues at the Max Planck Institute for Human Development in Berlin and

Robert Sternberg and his colleagues at Yale University. There is much overlap between the way the two groups conceptualize wisdom and their research findings are often complementary:

- Baltes and his colleagues define wisdom as 'expertise in the conduct and meaning of life.' According to their theory, a wise person is someone who knows what is most important in life and how to get it. He or she knows what constitutes the meaningful life and how to plan for and manage such a life.[4]
- Sternberg's definition of wisdom stems from his 'balance theory of wisdom.' According to this theory, people are wise to the extent that they use their intelligence to seek a common good. They do so by balancing their own interests with those of other people and those of larger groups (family, community, country). Wise people can adapt to new environments, change their environments, or select new environments to achieve an outcome that includes but goes beyond their personal self-interest.[5]

Intuitive Wisdom tells us that it is not what happens to us but what we do with what happens to us that makes all the difference. We can't erase our past negative conditioning, but that doesn't mean we have to remain at the mercy of it. Neuroscientists tell us we can build new neural real estate by re-wiring our brain circuits with positive thoughts and inclinations. So, we do not have to remain prisoners of our past programming.

> The highest levels of thought are only prerequisites for wisdom. The possession of the high levels of knowledge does not in itself mean that a person is wise. Wisdom is a rare combination of attributes, with cognitive development being only one feature of the array.[6]
>
> (H. Marchand)

Strengthening Your Intuitive Wisdom

Here are some things you can do to strengthen your Intuitive Wisdom:

- ❏ *Become a student of life.* Study wherever you are. Have what you've underlined in books, collections of thoughts and quotes, and your own journal entries readily available to keep your mind growing.
- ❏ *Practice making quick decisions.* Start with small, seemingly unimportant issues, like what to order from a menu, then move up to bigger decisions, like whether or not to move ahead on a request by one of your employees, or which side to weigh in on during a project debate.
- ❏ *Use humor as a way to free yourself up to use your Intuitive Wisdom.* Laughter dispels gloom, depression, worry, pain and aggravation, and frees the mind to cultivate your Intuitive Wisdom. Use it as a quick way to switch emotional gears, and snap back into action!
- ❏ *See beyond the arrogance and stubborness of others.* These are often a mask for lack of confidence, lack of skill, or fear. Let your Intuitive Wisdom guide you in delving deeper, exploring issues, and asking open-ended questions.
- ❏ *Accept the pain and discomfort of confronting reality and finding "True North."* There is a wonderful quote that says, "Facts do not cease to exist because they are ignored." (And always remember that "facts" themselves must be questioned. Remember the coffee research.) As you "get real" and clarify your vision—your True North as a leader—you will find yourself instinctively knowing how to respond to issues, how to take actions congruent to your vision, and how to let go of things that are not working.
- ❏ *Capture what resonates.* Whenever you hear a jewel of wisdom that speaks to you, capture it. Hold on to those inspiring jewels that resonate with something deep within you. Refer to this collection when you need rejuvenation or reminders of who you really stand for as a leader.

- ❏ ***Do not overlook the small details.*** Intuitively Wise leaders know that nothing is trivial, because everything is connected to the whole. Sometimes a small detail can hold the key to a root cause of an issue, or be the trigger for a unique solution.
- ❏ ***Refuse to get bogged down in information.*** This may seem to be in conflict with the last item, but they really do go together. Unfortunately, society has replaced wisdom with information, and information is increasing in quantum leaps. However, much of the information we receive is incorrect or deceptive. Use your Intuitive Wisdom to cull through information, and identify what is relevant to you. Let go of the rest!
- ❏ ***Realize that knowledge and wisdom are two different things.*** Knowledge is important, but knowing how to use knowledge is to have wisdom. Intuitive Wisdom grows as we integrate our knowledge with our experience. This becomes increasingly important when faced with life and death decisions. Surgeons, police officers, fire fighters all need to make split-second decisions that have fatal results if they are incorrect. How do they do it? Experience does come into play, but it's more than experience. It's the ability to recognize symptoms and cues, then assess options with lightning speed. When you ask these professionals "How did you figure out what was wrong, or what to do?" the response you hear most often is "My gut! I just knew! "
- ❏ ***Pay attention to your intuition.*** Like any ability or muscle, hearing your inner wisdom is strengthened by doing it consistently and routinely.
- ❏ ***Be open to the unusual, the mystical, and surprises.*** Know that wisdom begins with wonder.
- ❏ ***Realize that there is wisdom of the head and wisdom of the heart.*** The real wisdom—the Core Ability of Intuitive Wisdom—is knowing which one to focus on, and when.

Trust in your inner knowing, the Wise Self within you. It is a Core Ability you can call in every day as a leader. There is never enough time to gather all the facts you need, talk to all the experts, and create decision trees to identify the best answer. In fact, as a leader you probably already know that the moment of absolute certainty never arrives. Too many people in leadership positions get stuck in paralysis of analysis, leaving their people to flounder amid missed deadlines and faulty expectations. As an Extraordinary Leader, you must learn to call on your Intuitive Wisdom, value it, and use it with confidence. You come prewired with an incredibly deep inner knowing. Use it to become an Extraordinary Leader.

> I failed my exam in some subjects, but my friend passed. Now he's an engineer in Microsoft and I am the owner.
> (Bill Gates)

The Ability & the Color: Summary

Intuitive Wisdom: An inner knowing. Uncommon sense. Intuition that provides an immediate understanding of something, without the need for conscious reasoning or proof.

The Color Yellow: Yellow is the color representing perception and understanding. It signifies the blend of experience and knowledge to create uncommon sense. Yellow is the color of Intuitive Wisdom. When you operate from that place of alignment, you are able to make wise choices, take appropriate risks, step into the unknown with confidence, and intuitively know what to do, as you are being true to the Extraordinary You!

Cultivating Your Intuitive Wisdom

*Sometimes I lie awake at night and ask,
"Where have I gone wrong?"
Then a voice says to me, "This is going to
take more than one night."*
(Charles M. Schultz, Peanuts cartoonist)

Laser Focus Technique:

Preparation:

Prepare for this Laser Focus experience by finding a quiet location where you will be uninterrupted. Sit in a comfortable position that you can hold for 20-25 minutes.

Take a few deep breaths, exhaling slowly between each breath. Without trying to force your breath in any way, allow it to find its own natural depth and rhythm. Always breathe through your nose. (That's assuming your nasal passages are clear and unobstructed. Otherwise breathe through your mouth.)

Allow your attention to focus either on the sensation of your breath coming and going through your nostrils, or on the rising and falling of your belly as you breathe. Give your full attention to the coming and going of your breath.

If you realize your attention has wandered, and you find yourself engrossed in thinking ahead or day-dreaming, simply acknowledge the ego's trespass, then gently but firmly bring your attention back to your breathing.

The Process:

Once you feel focused and relaxed, take a few moments to digest the following insight from Charles Roth: *Wisdom is gained from within, and we extract it from our own life experiences through the experiences of solitude and introspection. Wisdom is not gained through intellect, but through our inner nature. It is not gained from without but from within. Arrange to have times of solitude in your life. Solitude and privacy are the most suitable conditions for wisdom to arise.*

As you can see, this Laser Focus Technique takes Charles Roth at his word. It is asking you to enter into a time of solitude and privacy. It is affording you a time to connect with that part of you that is connected with your Core Self, the Extraordinry You.

In the next few moments focus on two things: your breathing and the quote above. Your breathing should be normal and rhythmical and your attention directed on internalizing Roth's explanation of wisdom.

Considering the import of Roth's treatment of wisdom, say softly to yourself, *"I am blessed with a high degree of wisdom."* Repeat that affirmation at least five times aloud, breathing easily as you do so. Realize that you have literally shut your eyes in order to see clearly.

Now, think to yourself: *I know how to use the knowledge I already have wisely.* Continue to run that positive statement through your head for a few moments.

Now, follow that up with this statement as you say it aloud, *"My wisdom is strengthened every time I use it for good."* Repeat that statement slowly a few times. Allow it to penetrate your psyche. Know that positive, life affirming statements like this enhance your ability to draw upon your inner wisdom.

Bring one of your hands up and place it over your heart. That's where your wisdom resides. Not in your head, but your heart. Silently bless the openness of your heart and the wisdom it affords you.

Realize that a life of wisdom is a combination of inner focus and purposeful actions. See the inner you and the outer you completely aligned. Dwell on that complementary relationship for the next few moments.

Concentrate on the following words one at a time, by focusing on their deeper meaning:

uncommon sense	inner genius
sound judgment	foresight
wisdom	discernment
inner knowing	laser focus

If any distracting thoughts or images intrude, thank them for sharing, take a deep breath, and refocus on the word you are concentrating on.

Become aware of any thoughts you receive that you sense are coming from your Intuitive Wisdom. Nonjudgmentally allow this wisdom to penetrate your consciousness and see how it applies to any issues you are currently experiencing.

As you feel yourself reaching an end to this process, become aware once again of your breathing. Open your eyes, breathe deeply, and spend a few moments with your journal, jotting down any insights or feelings you experienced during this Laser Focus activity.

Please do not rush through this process. Allow each phase of this Laser Focus technique to penetrate into your gray matter. You will find that the neural pathways will take the essence of each word to your neocortex and strengthen your frontal lobe. That's a good thing. It will increase your chances of connecting with the wise and discerning Extraordinary You.

Self-Directed Activity to Develop Your Intuitive Wisdom Core Ability: Catch Yourself

There's an old management leadership book called *One Minute Manager,* by Ken Blanchard. The key principle in the book encourages leaders to catch a person doing something right every day, and say something positive to reinforce it.

While the concept may seem a bit simplistic, the book has been a best seller since it came out in 1982! By the way, there is another book published in 2000, written by Rae Andre and Peter D. Ward, that may reinforce the importance of adding sincerity to that "one minute of praise." That book is entitled *The 59-Second Employee: How to Stay One Second Ahead of Your One Minute Manager!*

This Extraordinary You connection is called: Catch Yourself. It is a strategy to help you be more mindful and aware of what it feels like when you are connected to the Intuitive Wisdom springing from the Extraordinary You. Here's how it works:

Part 1: Catch Yourself Unconnected. Catch yourself the next time you say "I knew I should have ..." It may be a phone call you wish you'd made, or perhaps a wish that you'd taken the extra time to review your report before you hit send, or maybe a realization you should have taken a different route to work as you sit in a traffic jam.

As soon as you hear yourself say, "I knew I should have..."—take a moment and pay attention to how you are feeling. Ask yourself these two questions:

- What was I feeling when I originally had the other thought? (i.e., what was I feeling when I thought about making the call; giving a second review; taking a different route?)
- What was I feeling when I chose to ignore that thought?

Now take a moment to realize the original feeling was your Intuitive Wisdom, giving you guidance about the situation. Remember again how you felt, and thank your Intuitive Wisdom for the guidance. Remind yourself that in the future you will be more open to following your intuitive guidance, even if you do not understand it at the time.

Part 2: Catch Yourself Connected! Ever had one of those moments when you listened to your intuition? How about a time when you went through a difficult or emotional experience, and handled it with grace? This is not just a coincidence or fluke. *(Read that last sentence again for emphasis! I'll wait!)* It happened because, in that moment, you were connected with the Extraordinary You, and you paid attention to the guidance from your Core Ability of Intuitive Wisdom. Part 2 of this activity invites you to stop the minute you catch yourself connected! In that moment, do two things:

- Notice how it feels. Awareness is the first step toward transforming a one-shot occurrence into a habit you can replicate over and over again! So pay attention to how the inner guidance feels, and how you responded to it.
- Honor yourself for being connected. People tend to repeat behavior they are rewarded for, so give yourself emotional kudos for following your intuition and getting great results!

The more you reinforce your ability to listen to your Intuitive Wisdom, the easier it is to call on it when you need it. Why not make your phenomenal wisdom your permanent personal and leadership address?

Using the Color Yellow:

If you want to strengthen your awareness of your Intuitive Wisdom, make yellow your color of focus. Choose to wear something yellow as part of your wardrobe; eat foods that are yellow in color (i.e., bananas, yellow squash, lemons); place items that are yellow in your environment (yellow flowers, a yellow stone, pictures with yellow being the dominant color).

While this may feel a little silly at first, allow yourself to give it a try without judgment. Become aware of how much more often you listen to your intuition; how much stronger your decisions become; how easily you know how to handle a situation, and how you are experiencing more Intuitive Wisdom in your life.

Intuitive Wisdom

Personal Reflections

*Date:*_____

Chapter 3: Inner Strength

The hard thing isn't setting a big, audacious, hairy goal. The hard thing is laying people off when you miss the big goal. The hard thing isn't hiring great people. The hard thing is when those "great people" develop a sense of entitlement and start demanding unreasonable things. The hard thing isn't setting up an organizational chart. The hard thing is getting people to communicate within the organization that you just designed. The hard thing isn't dreaming big. The hard thing is waking up in the middle of the night in a cold sweat when the dream turns into a nightmare."
(Ben Horowitz, in The Hard Thing About Hard Things:
Building a Business When There Are No Easy Answers)

When you develop Inner Strength as one of your core leadership qualities, you will be able to meet any challenge, disappointment, or difficulty with a high degree of confidence and poise. This Core Ability is the epitome of grit, resilience, mental toughness, tenacity, determination, and fortitude—which you already possess at a deep level.

Having strong Inner Strength allows you to draw on your internal resources, your mental skills, and your physical capabilities to confront difficulties of all kinds. And we all know that leadership brings its own barrage of difficulties! Embodying tenacity allows you to call on your energy and stamina, so when you face challenges that deplete you of energy and material resources, you still have enough willpower and grit left within you to act confidently and decisively.

I intentionally chose the opening quote to this chapter even though it is rather long for a chapter starter. To me, it sums up the problem with a lot of leadership development materials. The focus is on formulas and how-to models to handle the basic situations a leader may face (i.e., hiring, performance reviews, project planning, team development), while failing to encourage the deeper role of a leader which goes way beyond formulas and models. This is the heart of an Extraordinary Leader. It involves digging deep into that reservoir of experience, emotion, and inner strength to call forth the best in yourself and others, especially during stressful times. It spurs people to keep moving forward when the general desire is to quit, throw in your cards, and fold.

Inner strength is the internal engine that can move you toward the successes and achievements you want—for yourself and the people who report to you. It is the mental and emotional muscle that helps you accomplish what you want in life. Inner Strength, also called mental toughness, is erroneously considered as a quality belonging only to high-performing athletes who depend on strength and force to achieve their goals. The truth is, Inner Strength can be developed by everyone, because it is already within us, just waiting to be cultivated. It is one of the core abilities that will help you discover (uncover) the Extraordinary Leader you can be!

Inner Strength was the most difficult Core Ability to label, because it encompasses such a multitude of elements. LaRae Quy, former FBI conterintelligence and undercover agent, says it this way: "As [a leader] you need to be psychologically prepared to deal with strong competition, recover from mistakes and failure quickly, tackle tough situations, devise strategies, and collaborate with others."[1]

Willpower, which is inner strength in high gear, manifests as the ability to control unnecessary and harmful impulses. It also manifests as the ability to make decisions, abide by those decisions, and follow them with perseverance, until you successfully accomplish what you want to do. Leaders who have a low level of inner strength succumb to what Daniel Goleman calls 'emotional hijacking.' What happens is that small stresses pile up over time and cause many leaders to lose control. As a result, their decision-making skills, productivity, and effectiveness plummet.[2]

Inner Strength

You've seen it happen. You're in a meeting that seems to be going well, then suddenly someone says something that hits a sore spot, and someone goes emotionally berserk! Their reaction is totally inappropriate in relation to the incident. What happened was 'emotional hijacking' and it impacts everyone!

When a leader is unable to control emotions, employees become fearful, unsure, and unwilling to be creative or to present unpopular information needed for accurate decision making. Inner strength gives you, the leader, the courage and moxie to endure and overcome any and all resistance and opposition, difficulties and hardships. Mental toughness makes you emotionally resilient and provides an exceptional model for your people.

The following guidance from America's thirtieth President, Calvin Coolidge, is rich in perspective and gets to the heart of unwavering resolve:

> *Nothing in the world can take the place of persistence. Talent will not; nothing is more common than unsuccessful [people] with talent. Genius will not; unrewarded genius is almost a proverb. Education will not; the world is full of educated derelicts. Persistence and determination alone are omnipotent. The slogan "Press On" has solved and always will solve the problems of the human race.*

How many times have you wished you had more Inner Strength (willpower, self-discipline, tenacity, resolve, grit)? How many times have you lacked enough persistence and inner stamina to follow through on your decisions and plans? Do you admire and respect strong leaders who have overcome obstacles and difficulties because of the inner strength they possessed? Do you admire the fact that they had more willpower than won't power; that they were more disciplined than lackadaisical; that they perservered despite traumatic childhood experiences or tragedies as an adult?

Take heart! There are actions you can take to cultivate and fortify the Inner Strength that is one of your inherent Core Abilities. Through commitment, practice, and — well, Inner Strength — you will begin to see dramatic effects immediately. You will act more like an Extraordinary Leader, and your people will become more creative, communicative, engaged, and resilient as well.

> The secret of resiliency is going beyond tapping your own well of heartfelt positivity and being open to drink from what springs from others.[3]
> (Barbara Frederickson)

What Does Science Say?

Within positive psychology, resilience or resiliency is used to describe having an above normal positive capacity to cope with stress and adversity. It also refers to the ability to overcome and get over tough psychological experiences easier than the average person. That's what this Core Ability is all about.

Inner Strength is the ability to reject instant gratification or pleasure in favor of something more meaningful and growth-oriented. It manifests as the mental toughness to stick to actions or plans in spite of obstacles, difficulties, or unpleasantness. The more leaders work themselves up into a worried tizzy in anticipation of possible negativity, the slower they are to appreciate they have in fact dodged a bullet, so to speak. For leaders with resilient personality styles, less worry means faster relief.[4]

When tough times trigger your insecurities, you can call upon your Inner Strength to get you through anything the world throws at you with poise and confidence. My term for confidence is "poised courage."

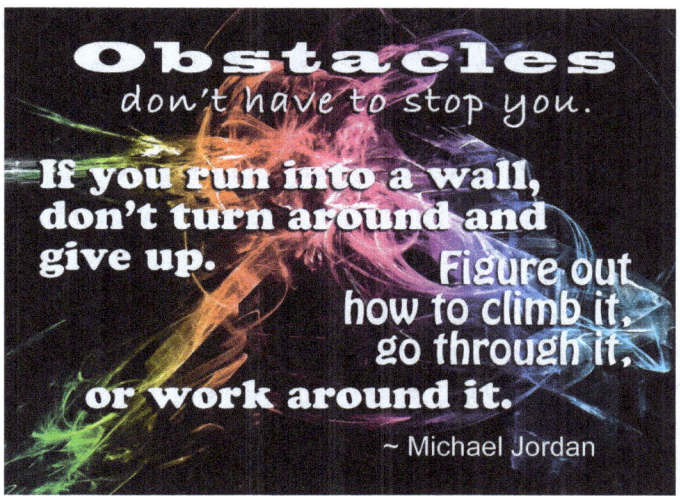

A compelling amount of research from the field of positive psychology tells us that all of us have these qualities. All of us are born with more unique capabilities and skills than we realize, and the way to build our Inner Strength is to focus on all seven Core Abilities and 'grow' them.

Someone who mastered stick-to-itiveness was Steve Jobs, who said:

Your work is going to fill a large part of your life, and the only way to be truly satisfied is to do what you believe is great work. And the only way to do great work is to love what you do. If you haven't found it yet, keep looking. Don't settle. As with all matters of the heart, you'll know when you find it. And, like any great relationship, it just gets better and better as the years roll on. So keep looking until you find it. Don't settle.

Inner Strength is deeper than just "bouncing back" from a difficulty or having 'tough skin.' One final piece of research coming from Harvard Graduate School of Education's Inner Strengths of

Successful Leaders program defines it well, and speaks to the essence of Extraordinary Leadership:

Inner strength deepens your presence, wisdom, focus, and ability to stay calm and centered. It helps you better manage uncomfortable feelings and difficult interactions, think more clearly and compassionately, discern where to direct your time and energy, sustain your enthusiasm, and achieve results.

These inner strengths help you take stress in stride, make wise decisions, and savor the joy of leadership. Through guided mindfulness practices and exercises, meditation techniques, case studies, reflection, presentations, role playing, and large and small group discussion, you gain new perspectives on your inner strengths and renew your commitment to action guided by the values that inspire you to make a difference.

Inner strength helps you identify common patterns of overreaction, and then learn how to respond to difficulties with awareness, poise, and resilience. It helps you respond deliberately rather than react automatically, to be guided by your values rather than be derailed by your discomfort. It helps you explore skills for self-awareness and self-renewal so that you can sustain your leadership and service to others with insight, wisdom, and warmth—and renew your incredible capacity for joy.[5]

When your Inner Strength is at its best, it generally shows up with these characteristics:

1. A clear conscious choice has been made.
2. Commitment, resolve, and stick-to-itiveness are present. You will not give up on a commitment no matter what mood, emotions, or roadblocks you might be facing.
3. Intentions are sharply defined and are not influenced by counter intentions and doubts.
4. A strong purpose fuels your willpower.
5. Your frustration tolerance is high. You can stand anything and are not easily overwhelmed despite appearances.
6. You see meaning and substantial value in what's to be done, and are not deterred by obstacles.
7. You make conscious choices by weighing the pros and cons of your undertakings.

> **Putting It Into Practice:**
>
> Take a moment to reflect back on a difficult work experience you went through recently. Be sure you think about something that is complete.
>
> How were you able to work through it?
>
> What lessons did you bring from the experience that have made you stronger?

Leaders who have a well-defined sense of Inner Strength are able to see through uncertainty and chaos. They remain calm in the midst of a troubled world, and can move through difficult situations with ease and grace. As a result, they are able to help their people do the same. When a situation appears to be chaotic, an Extraordinary Leader can bring his/her people together and bring reason and sense to what's happening.

Your employees respond to the signals you send out, and will follow your lead. Allowing a moment to talk about what's happening, identifying the obstacles, and inspiring people to move through the difficulties is true Inner Strength for uncertain times: the strength to risk reaching out; the strength to risk listening, hearing, holding, and understanding. The Inner Strength for outer action is in your DNA.

I can tell you with absolute certainty that you have a deep reservoir of Inner Strength within you. And when you align your ordinary self with your Extraordinary Self, you'll not only achieve a greater success as an Extraordinary Leader; you will achieve the inner peace and happiness that comes from being in alignment with the Extraordinary You.

Strengthening Your Inner Strength

Here are 15 specific actions you can take immediately to begin developing your Inner Strength, so it is available at the moment you need it.

1. End each day with a Gratitude List.

Counting your blessings, rather than your burdens, helps you keep life in a proper perspective. It reminds you of what is going right, which opens you up to options and creative solutions, as well as fuels the energy to stay the course.

2. Trust and honor your own personal power.

When you realize you are feeling victimized or undermined, in that moment refuse to give negative people or upsetting circumstances any power. By consciously refusing to blame anyone else for any setbacks or disappointments you experience, you harness your inner power of control and choice.

3. Accept challenges.

View adversity as an opportunity, even a catalyst, to grow stronger. With each obstacle you overcome, you gain confidence in your ability to become better. Seek out challenges as a way to srengthen this confidence.

4. Focus on the things you *CAN* control.

Rather than waste energy worrying about a problem or what might happen, invest your time and resources into preparing for what the situation. Whenever you are feeling like things are going bonkers, pause, take a deep breath, and ask youself, "What can I take control of in this situation?"

5. Set realistic and healthy boundaries.

Creating healthy emotional and physical boundaries gives you the room you need to grow. This means knowing what is yours to do, and what belongs to others. It also means being aware of who your "crazy-makers" are, and not allowing them to manipulate you.

6. Take calculated risks.

Leadership requires risk-taking, but not to the point of endangering the people or business for whom you are responsible. Practice balancing your emotions with logic so you can calculate each risk you face. Even when you step outside of your comfort zone, seek legitimate opportunities that will help ensure your success. Don't be afraid of a little discomfort or delayed gratification.

7. Make peace with the past.

You strengthen your Inner Strength every time you reflect on the past in order to learn from it. Let go of grudges and resentments, recognizing you can give a powerful meaning to everything that has happened.

8. Don't make the same mistake twice.

Rather than beat yourself up for your mistakes, focus on learning from them. Accept full responsibility for your choices and actions, and choose to move forward in a productive manner.

9. Define what success looks like for you, and celebrate the successes of others.

Rather than resent other people's good fortune, be a leader who makes it a habit to share in other people's successes and joys. Recognize that other people's achievements do not in any way diminish your own.

10. Set aside time for inner focus and introspection.

Strengthen your Inner Strength by taking time to collect your thoughts. Whether you write in a journal, meditate, or simply sit silently and reflect, invest in a 'retreat forward' into solitude—it is essential to your well-being.

11. Accept full responsibility for your choices and actions.

Rather than pine over your inaction, tap into your Inner Strength to create opportunities for yourself. Don't waste time waiting for the world to give you what you think you're owed. Take action to make something positive happen.

12. Persevere and be a master at stick-to-it-tiveness.

Understanding that the best things in life are worth waiting for, use your Inner Strength to exercise patience, poise, and practicality as you strive for goals that are meaningful.

13. Expand your mental energy wisely.

Leaders who trust their Inner Strength devote their energy to productive tasks. Don't waste limited resources, like time and energy, on things that aren't helpful.

14. Choose to be optimistic and positive as a general practice.

Leaders who rely on their Inner Strength talk to themselves like a trusted confidant. Refuse to believe in pessimistic or fatalistic predictions. Don't allow yourself to become overconfident, careless, or reckless.

15. Stay true to your values.

Leaders who consistently honor their Inner Strength keep their priorities in line with their beliefs and values. Be courageous enough to honor your integrity and authenticity, even when your choices may not be the most popular choices.

The Ability & the Color: Tip Sheet

Inner Strength: The inner fortitude to dig deep within yourself in order to handle challenging situations. Tenacity, resilience, stick-to-it-iveness, depth of conviction, and determination all define the meaning of Inner Strength, which has nothing to do with the size of your muscles. You can call on Inner Strength when you must move through a difficult task, or walk by a bowl of M&Ms!

The Color Russet Brown: Russet Brown is the color of stability, depth, and tenacity. It signifies strength and maturity. Russett Brown is the color of Inner Strength because it signifies your roots, which go deep within your being and allow you to accomplish things that may appear difficult, challenging, or even impossible, knowing you are claiming the Extraordinary You!

Extraordinary Leadership

Cultivating Your Inner Strength

Most people achieved their greatest successes one step beyond what looked like their greatest failure.
(Brian Tracy)

Laser Focus Technique:

Preparation:

Prepare for this Laser Focus experience by finding a quiet location where you will be uninterrupted. Sit in a comfortable position that you can hold for 20-25 minutes.

Take a few deep breaths, exhaling slowly between each breath. Without trying to force your breath in any way, allow it to find its own natural depth and rhythm. Always breathe through your nose. (That's assuming your nasal passages are clear and unobstructed. Otherwise breathe through your mouth.)

Allow your attention to focus either on the sensation of your breath coming and going through your nostrils, or on the rising and falling of your belly as you breathe.

Give your full attention to the coming and going of your breath.

If you realize your attention has wandered, and you find yourself engrossed in thinking ahead or day-dreaming, simply acknowledge the ego's trespass, then gently but firmly bring your attention back to your breathing.

The Process:

In your mind's eye formulate an image of a huge knot. As you examine it more closely, you discover that it is composed of hundreds of shoe laces that are tied together very tightly in the form of a knot the size of a basketball.

The knot is composed entirely of knots tied upon knots, so that the entire knot is constructed of over 1,000 knots.

Before the laces became a knot, they were soaked in a basin of water and then tied tightly and methodically into the massive knot of shoe laces you see before you.

Your mental task is to completely unravel the giant knot, one knot at a time.

Start by thinking to yourself, *"I am more tenacious than you,"* as you address the imaginary knot. Repeat that resoluteness five times to yourself.

Now, say aloud, *"I have tremendous fortitude and Inner Strength,"* as you address the imaginary knot again. Repeat that resolve five times aloud.

Notice how you are breathing. Make sure your breathing is normal and rhythmical. Keep the image of the tightly compressed knot in mind as you control your breathing.

Now, with your full and undivided attention on the mental knot, begin to see each knot on its surface begin to unravel, one at a time, so that the knot next to it is unraveled, and then the next knot is unraveled, and so on.

Continue to see each vice-like knot loosen and then unravel as you move around the circumference of the massive knot. Although it's a slow process (after all, the knot is composed of over 1,000 smaller knots), you are patiently and methodically untying each knot. Breathe easily as you do this.

Strands of loosely-layered shoe strings are beginning to collect next to the knot—which is shrinking because of your mental resolve.

Continue to breathe easily and normally as you untie each knot. See yourself untying even the tightest of the shoe lace knots with patience and poise.

Mentally see yourself close to untying the entire matrix of smaller knots. The pile of unraveled shoe laces is now much higher and broader than what's left of the once massive knot.

In your mind's eye, see the entire knot of shoe laces completely unraveled. Take a deep breath, exhaling slowly as you do so. Now, take another, then another.

Whisper to yourself, *"I epitomize unwavering resolve. I am tenacious. I am very determined."*

With your eyes still closed say aloud softly, *"I have unwavering resolve. My stick-to-itiveness is legendary. I am a pillar of determination."*

Allow a smile to form across your face. With eyes still shut, remind yourself that Inner Strength is one of your Core Abilities. It will sustain you and fortify you when you meet seemingly insurmountable challenges and obstacles.

Think about a time you may have gotten tied up into knots over something. Are you stifled by any emotional knots presently? Are you straightjacketed by any personal or professional self-defeating habits, attitudes, or assumptions? Are you facing any difficult project or personal challenge that feels overwhelming?

No matter how tightly you are bound by any of these limiting factors, see yourself resolutely overcoming each of them—just as you overcame the tightness of each of the shoe lace knots.

Say aloud, *"I have tremendous Inner Strength. I am tenacious. I am resilient. I am a pillar of determination."* Repeat those affirmations at least five times, paying attention to the sound of your voice as you do so. Repeat them as long as it takes for you to sense that you are repeating them with a confident tone of voice.

Each time you affirm your unwavering resolve, your moxie, your tenacity, your reservoir of Inner Strength, you tighten the connection between the ordinary you and the Extraordinary You. And that is a good thing—a very good thing!

Self-Directed Activity to Develop Your Inner Strength Core Ability: A Voice From the Past

This self-directed activity is one you can repeat as often as you like, and every time it will strengthen your Inner Strength Core Ability by reinforcing the ways you have used it successfully. Here's the process:

Part 1: Take a moment to think back over your past, and recall a situation when something was not going well. (Most people don't have any trouble coming up with something—the problem usually is narrowing it down to one thing! That's why you can do this activity numerous times, using a different situation each time.) For this experience, focus on one event from your past. Since we are focusing on Extraordinary Leadership, you probably want to choose a past emotional experience related to work, a tough situation handling an employee, a difficult decision related to a project, a poor decision you made ... any situation will do. Just be sure it is something from your past that has since been resolved or released, not something you are still dealing with emotionally.

Part 2: Got a handle on the specific experience? Describe it briefly in your journal or on a sheet of paper. No need to get emotional and detailed; simply describe it clearly enough that you know what the situation was and the impact it had on you as you

were going through it. Use the following questions to guide your decription:
- How would I describe this situation in two sentences?
- Who else was involved?
- What were my emotional reactions at the time?

Part 3: Now let this voice from the past speak to you from a new perspective. As you look back on this experience, reflect on how you see it differently. Jot down responses to the following questions:
- How do I see this situation in the context of where I am now?
- What lessons was I able to learn from this situation that have helped me?
- How am I different as a result of the way I handled this situation?
- If I could go back and move through this situation again, is there anything I would do differently? If so, what and why?

Part 4: Connect the "voice from your past" to your current time and situation. Jot down your thoughts as you reflect on these questions:
- What specific message can I take away from the "voice from my past?"
- What skills of Inner Strength, Resilience, Confidence, and Persistence did I use then that I now know are accessible for any current situation I face?
- What is a one-sentence phrase I can use to remind me of my Core Ability of Inner Strength, based on what this "voice from my past" has taught me?

What an empowering realization to know that, no matter how tough the road, you have what you need to move forward—and there are always ways you can use any situation for good. Claim your Inner Strength now, and know you possess incredible tenacity, resolve, and resilience.

Using the Color Russet Brown:

If you want to strengthen your awareness of your Inner Strength, make russet brown your color of focus. Choose to wear something brown as part of your wardrobe; eat foods that are brown in color (i.e., nuts, brown rice, beef, chocolate, coffee); place items that are brown in your environment (wooden sculptures, pine cone arrangement, a brown stone, pictures with brown being the dominant color).

While this may feel a little silly at first, allow yourself to give it a try without judgment. Become aware of how much more tenacious and resilient you are; how much stronger your actions become; how easily you are able to see projects through to the end, and how you are experiencing more Inner Strength in your life.

Extraordinary Leadership

Personal Reflections

Date:_____

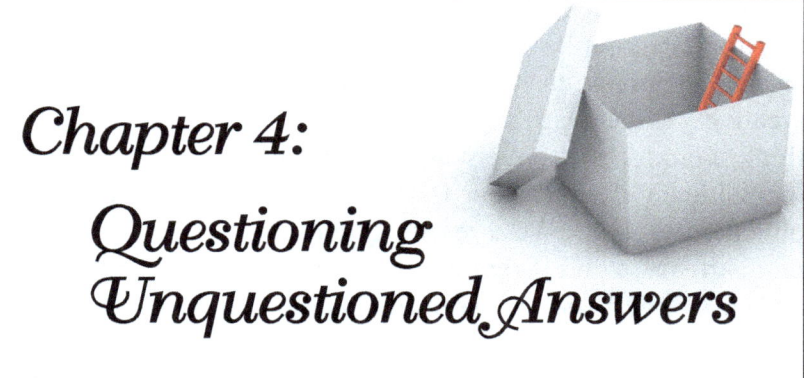

Chapter 4: Questioning Unquestioned Answers

If the spirit of wonder stays alive in us, we will always have new questions, & expand our creativity in response.
(Jay Woodman)

Questioning Unquestioned Answers, (also known as thinking outside-the-box) is a Core Ability that encourages you to step outside the norm, challenge the status quo, think unconventionally, and view everything from a new, expanded perspective. It encourages you to question everything you believe to be a fact, or a required way of doing things. What I'm actually recommending is for you to change a period to a question mark as you problem-solve and innovate. For example, suppose someone says "This information cannot be shared with our employees." It's time to change the period to a question mark: "This information cannot be shared with our employees?" Perhaps it's true, but maybe it's only an old legacy policy that no longer makes sense in your new culture that triumphs transparency.

Question everything that appears to be set in concrete! As an Extraordinary Leader, your skill in calling upon this Core Ability on a regular basis will set you apart and allow you to be innovative and productive in everything you do. You will discover new levels of creativity in yourself, and pull out the creativity of your people. As a result, you will see employee engagement soar!

So often when I introduce this Core Ability, I hear leaders collectively groan! The common response is, "Are you kidding? I can't question authority like that! And by the way, I'm not even creative." If that was the first thought you had, I encourage you to think again! Creativity is an inborn ability within each of us, including YOU! It's in our DNA. We all have the ability to think outside the box. We are all gifted with a high degree of inquisitiveness and ingenuity. Research says we are all born with an innovative bias. We naturally seek creative solutions to life situations that seem unsolvable and hard to figure out. We have the innate ability to understand incomprehensible problems, human dilemmas, and concepts. And it all starts with our Core Ability of Questioning Unquestioned Answers!

Think about this: When you were younger, did you ever lie back on the cool grass with a trusted friend on a hot summer day, enjoying the gentle breeze of summer caressing your face? Did you look up at the clouds and daydream? As you both looked up at the clouds, what did you see? Did you see more than clouds? Perhaps you saw a face in the clouds, an animal, or even an entire scene. If you had this kind of experience, you were using your Questioning Unquestioned Answers Core Ability. Instead of the statement "These are just clouds" you were posing a question: "These are just clouds?" That allowed you to see beyond the obvious.

Our oldest ancestors looked up at the stars and imagined seeing lions, water bearers, scorpions, and twins. The innovators who created amazing breakthoughs such as microwave ovens, search engines, smartphones, driverless cars, and individual-serving coffee makers were all questioning the traditional way of doing things. In fact, these days it seems whatever need we have, some out-of-the-box thinker has created a tool that allows us to say, "There's an app for that!"

What Does Science Say?

From the perspective of neuroscience, a chief characteristic of an inquiring mind is thought to be psycho-spatial processing. Psycho-spatial processing is when we conceive of an object, say a cube, in our mind's eye and then, in our mind, we move and rotate the cube. It is when we encounter and internalize an object from the external world, creating the mental representation of the thing we're looking at rather than the  object itself. Psycho-spatial processing is important, because it's how we pick up on patterns, which are then transferred via the corpus callosum to the left brain, where that information is logically processed and interpreted into familiar functions such as language and mathematics.

There's an important point to be made here: creativity is NOT simply the perceptual and processing capacities of the right hemisphere; it is the combination of perception, processing, transmission, and integration of information from one hemisphere to the other. An inquisitive mind is a neuroplastic (natural adaptive/developmental) process, facilitated by specific brain regions that can be intentionally driven and developed. Questioning "facts" and traditionally accepted ways of doing things is a skill that can be acquired and optimized by systematically targeting cognitive processes which traverse the corpus callosum—causing the neurons of the left and right hemispheres to fire and wire together, a process known in neuroscience as the *Hebbian postulate*.[1]

In their book *Super Brain*, Deepak Chopra and Rudolph Tanzi talk about the mind/brain connection, and share that with neuroimaging, scientists can now track every thought in your brain. From a leadership perspective, it's interesting to note that when employees are experiencing extreme stress at work, the sympathetic nervous system is on overdrive, which can lead to exhaustion and illness. However, Chopra amd Tanzi take an interesting perspective of this information. "It would be a mistake," they say, "to attribute the exhaustion and illness to our work, or to technology, or the demands of our life. It's our responsibility really, whether we feel stress or not. Stress is not in the environment, stress is not in you, it's how you and your environment interact. It's like the waves on the ocean. If you are a skillful surfer, then every wave is almost an exhilaration; if you're unprepared, then every wave is a disaster."[2]

So how does this relate to the Core Ability of Questioning Unquestioned Answers? Encouraging this kind of questioning—and providing the opportunity to practice it—creates a safe environment where employees can comfortably be innovative, productive, creative, and relaxed. Leaders who model the art of Questioning Unquestioned Answers reduce stress and tension, and open the door for productive interaction between the environment and the individuals he/she is leading.

One of the great philosophers of all time, Dr. Seuss, described Questioning Unquestioned Answers this way: "Think left, think right, think low, think high. Oh, the thinks you can think up if only you try!"

As I thought right and as I thought left, I thought of a quote by Albert Einstein: "Imagination," he says, "is more important than knowledge. Knowledge is limited to all we know and understand while imagination is the preview of coming attractions."

The out-of-the-box thinking I'm talking about is the process of challenging what psychologists call *confirmation biases*. A confirmation bias means that once we have formed a certain viewpoint, we accept information that confirms to that view and ignore (or downright reject) any information that casts doubt on it. A strong confirmation bias suggests that we may not perceive circumstances objectively. We pick out those bits of data that make us feel good because they confirm our current belief system. Thus, we become prisoners of our assumptions. (Remember the "facts about coffee" example in Chapter 2?)

When we are stuck in our confirmation biases, we tend to use *convergent thinking*, a term coined by Joy Paul Guilford. Convergent thinking involves aiming for a single, correct solution to a problem (similar to giving the "right" answer on a standardized test), while *divergent thinking* involves questioning the obvious, seeking creative, out-of-the-box generation of multiple answers to a particular problem.[3]

How many times have you been involved in a meeting where a problem is identified, an idea for solution is presented, and everyone immediately focuses in on all the reasons the solution won't work: no budget; limited time; stretched resources? These

Questioning Unquestioned Answers

stale excuses feed the confirmation biases in the room, and stifle any potential for innovation solutions. This is the time for you to call upon your Core Ability of Questioning Unquestioned Answers to dramatically change the conversation—and the results!

The distinct advantage of challenging traditional answers is that it keeps us out of a thinking dilemma called the *Einstellung Effect*. The Einstellung Effect (a classic case of convergent thinking) refers to our predisposition to accept traditional solutions even though "better" or more appropriate methods of solving the problem exist. It's very similar to the paralysis by analysis conundrum. Ever experience that while working with a team?

Before I get too carried away with my out-of-the-box thinking, however, I want to make one thing perfectly clear: both 'inside-the-box' and 'outside-the-box' thinking are necessary and prudent forms of using our gray matter. So, the process of thinking "inside the box" (convergent thinking) need not be construed in a negative sense. It is crucial for a variety of tasks, such as making decisions, analyzing data, and 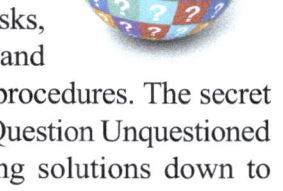 managing the progress of standard operating procedures. The secret of Extraordinary Leaders is knowing when to Question Unquestioned Answers and when to move on to narrowing solutions down to actionable steps for implementation. It's the creative dance Extraordinary Leaders perform on a daily basis.

Strengthening Your Core Ability of Questioning Unquestioned Answers

Let's think about the proverbial box for a moment, and then let's figure out how to climb out of it. What is the box that people are always talking about? The box is a conventional framework, a traditional way of thinking about things. In business, we are very good at in-the-box thinking because business is structured around the 'box' (the standard operating procedures). When you think about it, convergent in-the-box thinking is a break it/fix it model, and it's not known for generating radically new or interesting solutions to vexing problems.

Thinking outside the box is more than just a business cliché. It means approaching problems in innovative ways—looking at things from unusual perspectives. It implies an ability to conceptualize problems differently, and invites you to explore your position in relation to any particular situation in ways you'd never thought of before. Ironically, it's a cliché that means to think of clichéd situations in ways that aren't, well, clichéd.

Check Yourself for Confirmation Bias Habits

It's time to get personal! Here are just a few habits that interfere with your skill at drawing on your Core Ability to Question Unquestioned Answers. Check yourself out and see how many of these habits might be affecting you in your leadership role. (Here's a little tip: This is only useful if you are completely honest! If you're not sure, have a trusted colleague who knows you well complete it for you!) Check the boxes that describe you.

❏ Negative attitude about any information that does not conform with your current beliefs.

- ❑ Fear of failure or criticism; perfectionism.
- ❑ Workplace stress, or unhealthy stress in general.
- ❑ A need to do it yourself or micromanage others to be sure the results are exactly what you expect and need.
- ❑ Rigidly following current rules and existing beliefs (not flexible, unable to perceive the value of gray areas).
- ❑ Making false assumptions—about others, about the world, about the situation, about the expectations you feel weighing on you, about your own talents and abilities.
- ❑ Over-reliance on traditional logic, along with assuming you have an accurate grasp of what is logical.

If you checked *any* of these boxes, I invite you to spend some time relaxing that mindset, then noticing the difference it makes in your overall effectiveness.

Check Yourself for Skill in Questioning Unquestioned Answers

Now it's time to see what habits you have as a leader that foster your being able to Question Unquestioned Answers. What follows are just a few ways you can increase your out-of-the-box thinking muscle. Check the ones that describe you as a leader. Again, if you're not sure, just ask a trusted colleague to critique you!

- ❑ ***Question everything:*** "Expert opinion," says Kuhn, "fouls up the creative engine."[4] Familiarity and routineness lead many people into frozen evaluations, straight-jacketed concepts, and boxed-in assumptions. Science is discovering that when you are curious about things, you trigger a cascade of reactions that light up the brain, while an incurious brain begins losing its effectiveness.[5]

    By inviting you to challenge existing beliefs and policies, I'm encouraging a departure from your organization's existing norms, values, and perception of limits. Expectation of conformity runs contrary to the spirit of creativity. Our inability to think outside the expected and accepted norms is becoming an epidemic! Ken Robinson argues that the current education system is "educating people out of their creativity."[6] That's why, as Extraordinary Leaders, it is essential to create a safe environment conducive to Questioning Unquestioned Answers.

❏ *Release the past:* There is an almost instinctive tendency of leaders and organizations to protect their past successes and rest on past laurels rather than separate themselves from convention or fading technologies. Peter Drucker refers to it as 'succumbing to the temptation to feed yesterday and starve tomorrow.'[7]

❏ *Know what to overlook:* Knowing what to overlook and focusing on the essence of the problem or task at hand are the driving forces that sustain our creative fires. Knowing what you are looking for helps you separate the vital few pieces of information from the trivial many as you search for new insights.

❏ *Listen to the voice of eccentricity within:* It has been argued by transpersonal psychologists, sociologists, and neuroscientists that there is an innate idiosyncratic knowing in all of us that defines our originality, imagination, and just plain common sense. So, heeding that idiosyncratic voice is a necessary aspect of our unfoldment, and certainly of our ability to be an Extraordinary Leader.

The neurobiology of creativity has been addressed in the article "Creative Innovation: Possible Brain Mechanisms." The authors write that "creative innovation might require coactivation and communication between regions of the brain that ordinarily are not strongly connected." Highly creative leaders who excel at creative innovation have an idiosyncratic knowing that defines their 'creative voice.' They tend to differ from others in three ways:

- they have a high level of specialized knowledge,

- they are capable of divergent thinking mediated by the frontal lobe,
- and they are able to modulate neurotransmitters such as norepinephrine in their frontal lobe. Thus, the frontal lobe appears to be the part of the cortex that is most important for creativity.[8]

❑ ***Travel off beaten paths:*** Traveling off beaten paths frees up the imagination and helps you gain perspectives that you wouldn't otherwise have if you "walled" yourself up in routineness and assumed "facts."

Incubation may amplify the process of creative problem-solving, as suggested in some empirical evidence consistent with the hypothesis that incubation enables "forgetting" of misleading clues. Absence of incubation may lead problem solvers to become fixated on inappropriate strategies of solving the problem.[9]

For Extraordinary Leaders, I am recommending more than just "taking a break" from your problem-solving. I invite you to travel off the beaten path of your expertise area and the departments you manage. Get to know other areas within your organization, and draw representatives into your problem-solving sessions who have no relationship to your area. You'll be amazed at the insights you get from fresh, unbiased eyes!

❑ ***Recognize patterns, tendencies, and trends:*** We are living in an age of discontinuities ... of cognitive dissonance ... of increasing ambiguity ... of unknown future events. Seeing relationships and inter-relationships between seemingly disparate things allows us to see order within chaos, rightness within absurdity, truth within ambiguity.

❑ ***Know when to say when:*** There are limits to everything. Some limits are real, others are assumed. In everything we do there seems to be a place at which doing, making, having, and avoiding stops. Pushing the envelope must be mediated by common sense and sound judgment. Seeing limits as merely suggestions, as springboards, is one of the keys to unlimited creativity.

❑ ***Develop a bias for creative loafing:*** This one is particularly tough for many leaders to grasp! But hear me out. Creativity requires work and play in order to court the Muse. Leisure time can be leverage time! The cycle of initial awareness, followed by an intense and prolonged courtship interrupted by a planned period of disinterest (creative loafing), electrifies the Muse. The art of questioning depends on a number of things: experience, including knowledge and technical skills; talent; an ability to think in new ways; and the capacity to push through uncreative dry spells.

Intrinsic motivation—being turned on by the work itself—is a powerful driver, but it often comes at a price. Employees who get caught up in the work they do truly believe they are most creative when they are working under severe deadline pressure. But a recent study of 12,000 aggregate days that Teresa Amabile and her research team followed showed just the opposite: Employees were the least creative when they were fighting the clock. In fact, they found a kind of time-pressure hangover—when people were working under great pressure, their creativity went down not only on that day but the next two days as well. Time pressure stifles creativity because people can't deeply engage with the problem. (By the way, this applies to leaders too!) Innovative approaches require an incubation period (creative loafing); people need time to soak in a problem and let the ideas bubble up.

In fact, it's not so much the deadline that's the problem; it's the distractions that rob people of the time to make that creative breakthrough. Employees and leaders alike can certainly be creative when they're under the gun, but only when they're able to focus on the work. They must be protected from distractions, and they must know that the work is important and that everyone is committed to it.[10]

According to Kenneth Heilman, a neurologist at the University of Florida and the author of *Creativity and the Brain* (2005), innovative, out-of-the-box solutions not only involve coming up with something new, but also with shutting down the brain's habitual response, or letting go of conventional solutions. There may be, for example, a dampening of norepinephrine, the neurotransmitter that sets off the fight-or-flight alarm *(I would add the word freeze—the inability to do anything)*. That's why creative connections often occur when people are peaceful and relaxed.[11]

❏ ***Welcome spontaneity and chance encounters:*** The literature on what I am calling Questioning Unquestioned Answers is filled with examples of how unplanned events led people to worthwhile discoveries and phenomenal innovative ideas. Many breakthrough moments are the result of chance encounters that integrate experience meeting opportunity. But don't take my word for this. Look up the historic "discoveries" of beloved staples such as chocolate chip cookies, potato chips, slinky, the pacemaker, corn flakes, and safety glass for a few examples.

❏ ***Ask what assumptions you are making:*** Because we are literally bombarded with sensory stimuli, we have to select out what we chose to pay attention to. And we make assumptions about everything based on those perceptual filters (our confirmation biases). So, our assumptive nature determines how we respond to our environment unless we actively and consciously question those assumptions. We can take the assumptive handcuffs off and clear our perceptual channels through the intentional monitoring of our thought processes.

Teaching employees to solve problems that do not have well defined answers is another way to foster their creativity. This is accomplished by allowing employees to explore problems, examine assumptions, and redefine them, possibly drawing on knowledge that at first may seem unrelated to the problem in order to solve it.[12]

❏ ***Recognize that success comes in cans, not cannots:*** I first heard this quote from Keynote Speaker Joel Weldon, who uses an actual can as his business card! The quote means having more willpower than won't power. It means not putting yourself in a position to confuse activity with accomplishment. It means, according to William Thompson, Chairman of California-based Thompson Vitamins, that innovators are people who have 'the ability not just of envisioning the future in an abstract, daydreaming, fantasizing kind of way, but have the interest and the capability and the drive to actually do something about it."[13]

❑ ***Sanction calculated risks:*** Because creativity is unfailingly riveted to the unknown and untried, it invariably involves risk. However, the risks do not have to be cavalier risks. As Geis reports, the really good out-of-the-box thinkers "turn leaps of faith into plays of percentage."[14]

These are just twelve of the thousands of ways you can enhance your ability to use your Core Value of Questioning Unquestioned Answers to be an Extraordinary Leader. The creative channels are only limited by your desire and ingenuity. I assure you that once you openly embrace your out-of-the-box thinking nature, you will be surprised at how prodigious you are at finding novel solutions to any and all situations and circumstances that toss curve balls at you.

The Goridan Knot Legend:

The Gordian Knot is a legend associated with Alexander the Great. It is often used as a metaphor for an intractable problem (disentangling an 'impossible' knot) solved easily by thinking outside the box (cutting the Gordian knot instead of trying to untie it).

As the legend goes, in 333 BC, while wintering at Gordium, Alexander the Great attempted to untie the Gordian knot. When he could not find the end of the knot to unbind it, he sliced it in half with a stroke of his sword, producing the required ends (the so-called 'Alexandrian solution'). Whether his solution was fact or fiction, it serves to remind us that there are many ways to solve knotty problems.

Questioning Unquestioned Answers

One of my favorite leaders who was good at "hitting curve balls" was Apple Inc.'s founder Steve Jobs. When Apple was going through one of their particularly difficult financial dives, he described his feelings about innovation: "The cure for Apple is not cost-cutting. The cure for Apple is to innovate its way out of its current predicament." I believe the same holds true for all of us: The cure for what challenges or ails us is to innovate our way out of any and all predicaments by Questioning Unquestioned Answers.

> **Putting it into Practice:**
>
> Choose at least two of the dozen ideas listed on the past few pages, and focus on integrating them into the way you lead for the next three weeks. Record your experiences in your Personal Reflections journal and pay attention to how these changes have impacted you and your work as a leader.

Leslie Pfaff captured the essence of what this Core Ability is all about when she said, "Creativity isn't just about being an architect or an artist; it's about how you use your mind. From the Stone Age innovator who took two flints and sparked fire, to the inventors who studied sand and conceived the silicon chip, out-of-the-box thinking has transformed the world we live in. And it's likely to be even more important in the coming decades, as we try to solve a host of complex problems: how to develop novel energy sources; bring peace to unstable regions; and find better and more affordable ways to treat diseases."[15]

Here's one more thing I encourage you to take to heart concerning this Core Ability: Remember that everyone has a right to their own opinion, but not their own facts. So question any and all unquestioned answers—and confirm the facts surrounding the situation. You will be on your way to becoming an Extraordinary Leader ... as you help all the people you lead connect with the Extraordinary Nature they possess.

The Ability & the Color: Summary

Questioning Unquestioned Answers: Challenging existing policies, procedures, habits, beliefs, and anything else that is accepted as a "given;" thinking outside-the-box; creativity and innovation; flexibility in thinking; seeing unique and unusual connections and solutions; non-conforming and risk-taking; an inquiring mind.

The Color Blue: Blue is the color representing self-expression and creativity. It signifies an ability to think beyond the predictable and known, and stretch into innovative solutions to situations. Blue is the color of Questioning Unquestioned Answers because when you operate from that place of alignment as a leader, you open your awareness to innovative ideas. You live in the awareness that you can always discover better ways to handle situations, come up with innovative solutions, and identify unique approaches to everything, as you remain true to the Extraordinary You!

Cultivating Your Core Ability of Questioning Unquestioned Answers

"Dream more than others think practical. Expect more than others think possible. Care more than others think wise." (Howard Schultz))

Laser Focus Technique:

Preparation:

Prepare for this Laser Focus experience by finding a quiet location where you will be uninterrupted. Sit in a comfortable position that you can hold for 20-25 minutes.

Take a few deep breaths, exhaling slowly between each breath. Without trying to force your breath in any way, allow it to find its own natural depth and rhythm. Always breathe through your nose (That's assuming your nasal passages are clear and unobstructed. Otherwise breathe through your mouth.)

Allow your attention to focus either on the sensation of your breath coming and going through your nostrils, or on the rising and falling of your belly as you breathe.

Give your full attention to the coming and going of your breath.

If you realize your attention has wandered, and you find yourself engrossed in thinking ahead or day-dreaming, simply acknowledge the ego's trespass, then gently but firmly bring your attention back to your breathing.

The Process:

Think to yourself: *In spite of my thoughts to the contrary, I am incredibly creative. My ingenuity and innovative spirit are limitless and unbounded.* Now, give yourself the same compliment out loud.

As thoughtfully as you can, say aloud each of the following phrases:

I question unquestioned answers

I challenge facts

I think outside-the-box

Repeat these phrases three times in succession. Now whisper, *"They all describe me!"*

For the next five minutes or so, focus on the affirmative phrase, *"I question unquestioned answers."* Think it. Say it. See it. Feel it. Hear it. Taste it.

Remind yourself that your extraordinary nature is natural. It's inborn. It's in your DNA. Whisper to yourself, *"Questioning and creativity are in my DNA."* Say it softly a number of times.

Picture your employees, colleagues, managers, friends, and family all saying, *"_____ (your name), you are so innovative."* Imagine their enthusiastic acknowledgement of your ingenius way of thinking. See yourself believing them and in their assessment of your creativity. Bask in the sound of the word 'creative' being used to describe you.

In your mind's eye, picture an image of a square box which has a closed lid. It can be any size box you want to envision. It can be made of any materials you desire, and any colors you chose. This box is meant to hold all the things that hold you back from taking risks, challenging norms, and thinking outside-the-box.

On the lid of the box are words describing what's in the box. Here are some of the words, although you can make up more if you like: fear of ridicule or losing my job, lack of support from my managers, financial setbacks, lack of productivity, faulty communication, sickness, betrayal, mistakes, unrealistic deadlines; false assumptions, missed opportunities, actively disengaged employees; overwork; unmet goals.

There are two things you should notice immediately: one is that all of the terms and short phrases are negatively-charged; and the second is that you are outside of the box imagining that it is there. You are thinking out-of-the-box and the negativity is inside the box.

Keeping your attention on your imaginary box, realize that when you place yourself outside of negative emotional enclosures, anything you think will be out-of-the-box thinking. It will not be subject to the limitations associated with negative outlooks. It will not be restricted by the confines of the consciousness that created it.

Say aloud, *"I solve many problems by thinking outside-the-box. I question everything that appears to be true."* Repeat the affirmations until you're clear that it really is true about you.

Pay attention once again to your breathing and to your sitting posture. If you find that your neck and shoulders are tense, relax them. Breathe easily and normally.

Now, imagine you are 20 years older than you are now. What would you be doing? Where would you be living? As you look back on your life, what one thing would you have done differently that would have improved your chances 20 years later of living a happy, healthy, joyful, productive life? [*Note: If this number puts you at an age beyond what you think is possible—GOOD! This is another opportunity to think outside the proverbial box!*]

Returning your awareness to your present life—how can you shape it, change it, modify it, correct it, amplify it, improve upon it now, to match the vision you had? What leadership behaviors could you change?

As you breathe easily and rhythmically, say to yourself, *"I am incredibly creative. I question unquestioned answers. I am an Extraordinary Leader."* Repeat these affirmations until you are satisfied that you are what you say you are!

Self-Directed Activity to Develop Your Questioning Unquestioned Answers Core Ability: How is My Issue Like . . .

This is a great activity to stretch your Core Ability of Questioning Unquestioned Answers while you generate potential solutions to a problem you are facing. All you need is a blank sheet of paper and a pen or pencil. Here's the process:

> Write your issue or problem at the top of a blank sheet of paper. Be as clear, concise, and specific in your problem statement as possible.
>
> Look around the room and quickly choose some object. It can be anything, from the paper clip on your desk to a spiral notebook on your shelf to the light switch on the wall. It doesn't matter what you choose. The key is to make a choice quickly, then stick with whatever you choose.
>
> Create a list describing as many aspects of the item you selected as you can. Push yourself to list at least 25 descriptors. For example, if you chose a paper clip, you might list things like: it only holds a limited number of papers; it is bright and colorful; it is flexible and can be bent in different shapes; it comes in a box with other similar clips; it can be reused; it could keep a hem together; it has different spiral sizes within it; it could be uncurled and used as a pipe cleaner; etc.
>
> Once you have a lengthy list of descriptive phrases, go back to your problem statement and force-fit each descriptor to your problem, suggesting possible solutions. Ask yourself: *How is my issue like this paper clip?*
>
> For example, if your problem is limited resources for a project, you could say my resources can only handle limited number of items ... so perhaps I need to prioritize what is most important to focus on; my project is bright—perhaps I can create a colorful presentation to convince funding help from others; what kinds of flexibility do I have in terms of

using other resources, or using a resource I already have in more than one way? You get the idea!

Continue jotting down your insights, then go back and review what you wrote. Focus on what ideas pop into your head to develop further as solutions.

> ### Using the Color Blue:
>
> If you want to strengthen your awareness of your Questioning Unquestioned Answers Core Ability, make blue your color of focus. Choose to wear something blue as part of your wardrobe; eat foods that are blue in color (you are allowed to be creative, especially with this Core Ability! Consider blueberries, blue M&Ms, blue corn chips, Blue Diamond almonds — and don't forget bleu cheese!); place items that are blue in your environment (blue flowers, a blue stone, pictures with blue as a dominant color). You can even use blue ink or markers when you write.
>
> While this may feel a little silly at first, allow yourself to give it a try without judgment. Become aware of how ideas seem to flow to you effortlessly, how much easier it feels to solve problems that crop up, and how you are experiencing more out-of-the-box thinking in your life.

Personal Reflections

Date: _____

Chapter 5: Optimistic Spirit

Optimistic people generally feel that good things will last a long time and will have a beneficial effect on everything they do. And they think that bad things are isolated; they won't last too long and won't affect other parts of life. (Martin Seligman)

How about a quick test to get us started with this Core Ability? Take a peek at the following four questions and respond with your immediate first impression. In your opinion:

- Is optimism beneficial or does it interfer with realistic action planning and productivity?
- Is optimism simply wishful thinking?
- Does optimism play an important role in leadership, or does it interfere with achieving bottom-line results?
- How would you describe your level of optimism as a leader, and what are three specific examples of how you have demonstrated it?

I believe when you read this brief treatment of the Core Ability of Optimistic Spirit, you will see the immense psychological, emotional, and health benefits—not to mention the leadership benefits—to cultivating this particular ability. You will see that an

Optimistic Spirit may not change the situation, but it can absolutely put things into a healthier, more life-affirming perspective that opens your mind to solutions, and puts you in a position to influence the behavior of your employees for enhanced results.

Being optimistic is an attitude that sees situations and events as being temporary and controllable, although the situation itself may not be fully understood. Optimism is characterized by an attitude of hope for future conditions unfolding in a beneficial way, as well as seeing the potential in situations and people even when it is not obvious. A broader view of optimism, well stated by Einstein, is the understanding that "our lives—past, present and future—operate by laws of optimization and that the universe is wired in our behalf." But the real question is, does it have a place in leadership? I would give a definitive YES response! Let's dig a little into science for some support!

What Does Science Say?

Positive psychologist Martin Seligman, Ph.D., founder of Positive Psychology, coined the term *optimalism* as a willingness to accept failure while remaining confident that success will follow. However, it doesn't mean looking at life with rose colored glasses. There is an objectivity to optimism and its sister term optimalism. Seligman expressed his strong viewpoint by saying, "What we want is not blind optimism, but flexible optimism! We must be able to use pessimism's keen sense of reality when we need it, but without having to dwell in its dark shadows."[1] His work has a strong message for leaders.

We've all heard research reporting that optimists have been shown to live healthier lifestyles, smoke and drink less, tend to be more active, handle stress more proactively, make lemonade out of lemons (as the saying goes), and tend to live longer, healthier lives. But wait! There's more—and it relates specifically to leaders.

Research confirms that optimistic leaders typically outperform pessimistic leaders in their ability to confront and deal with problems they encounter. Additionally, leaders with an Optimistic Spirit are more successful in creating an environment conducive to employee engagement, inspiring open communication, and positive feedback.[2]

So, if I seem overly enthusiastic about this Core Ability, it's because I'm, well, optimistic! And when you light up your rostral anterior cingulated cortex by being more optimistic, you'll take another important step closer to connecting with your Core Nature. I've got to tell you that there are mountains of data illustrating the benefits of being optimistic.

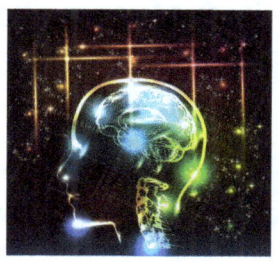

A study by Tali Sharot and colleagues from New York University asked participants to recall past events as well as imagine future ones based upon on-screen cues (such as winning an award or getting a hug). They were then asked to describe their thoughts—how strong, emotional, and positive each thought was, and whether or not the positiveness was experienced first-hand.

The results clearly demonstrated a rosier picture. Participants rated upcoming events more positively than they did happy past events—things they had actually experienced. Interestingly, participants viewed future events from a first-hand perspective if they were positive, but from an outsider's perspective if negative. Isn't that amazing!

Now, here's the neuroscience of optimism: As thoughts of happy future events flooded their minds, two brain structures were strongly activated. The rostral anterior cingulated cortex (RACC) and the right amygdala areas were lit up. The RACC, it seems, works hand-in-hand with our emotional center, the amygdala, to actually downplay negative emotions, helping us to stay more positive in the face of negative situations.[3]

Strengthening Your Core Ability of Optimistic Spirit

Here is just a handful of research tidbits packed with great 'how-to' tips to bolster your Optimistic Spirit, and thrive as you take advantage of the leadership benefits of optimism.

1. *Stamp indelibly on your mind a mental picture of yourself as succeeding in whatever you do.* Hold onto this mental scenario tenaciously. Over time your mind will imprint this optimistic perspective in the neural pathways of your brain. So always picture a successful outcome no matter how badly things seem to be going at the moment.

2. *Whenever a negative thought comes to mind, deliberately generate a positive thought to cancel it out.* This really works because of our brain's neuroplasticity (the lifelong ability to generate new neural real estate).[4]

3. *Do not manufacture obstacles in your imagination. Anesthetize every so-called obstacle.* Difficulties and challenges must be studied and efficiently dealt with to be eliminated, but they must be seen only for what they are. They must not be inflated by fear, doubt, anger, and false assumptions.

4. *Gain self-knowledge.* 'Know thyself,' as the saying goes. Learn the origin of your inferiorities, self-doubts, and vulnerabilities. If necessary, get a competent counselor to help you understand why you may have cultivated such a negativity bias.

5. *Believe in your own extraordinariness.* As you learn to become more optimistic, do not become egotistical, but develop a wholesome attitude of self-respect and self-confidence.

6. *Make your own luck.* I'm not kidding! It's easy to do since L.U.C.K. is an acronym which means 'Living Under Correct Knowledge.' Richard Wiseman, a psychologist from the University of Hertfordshire and

author of *The Luck Factor*, spent a decade researching people's perceptions of their luck. He found that those who call themselves lucky are more extraverted. That means they are more likely to have fortuitous encounters because they tend to keep in touch with a large support system. These optimistic folks also tend to be more open and flexible, and are less likely to experience negative emotional states like anxiety, anger, guilt, and depression. (Here's an interesting research tidbit: Across genders and ages, people born between March and August believe themselves to be luckier, on average, than those born in the colder months of September through February. Summer babies seem to grow up to be more open-minded and less neurotic than winter tots.[5])

7. ***Prime yourself for serendipitous experiences.*** Expect unexpected good fortune. It may come as a surprise, but conscientiousness is no friend to serendipity. Why? Because 'conscientiousness' means you "do what you're supposed to do, and you stick with it," explains Carol Sansone, professor of psychology at the University of Utah. The problem is, conscientious people will persist in a task even when there's no good reason to do so. By rigidly pouring all of your effort into one approach, you miss out on serendipitous paths to success that can be fulfilling and joyful. Good outcomes increase self-efficacy (the belief that you are capable of accomplishing whatever you set out to do). They also fuel an appetite for future risks. In other words, don't sell yourself short. [6]

8. ***Say 'yes' to opportunities.*** If you snooze you lose, as the saying goes. Some people's lives seem full of fortuitous circumstances, while others (the snoozers) are riddled with regrets about roads not taken. Instead of worrying about what could go wrong, give it a try. Even though some opportunities may slip away, there are always new ones coming along. Why? Because opportunities knock more than once, many times more than once.

9. ***Know that there is a difference between rational optimism and insane optimism.*** "Rational optimism," says Shawn Achor, author of *The Happiness Advantage*, is "a realistic assessment of the present, while maintaining a belief that our behavior will eventually create a better reality." Irrational optimist's ideas are usually Pollyannaish, delusional, and grossly flawed. They forget that reality is part of the formula that makes rational optimism work.[7]

> *If a setback is thought about as temporary, changeable, and local, that's optimism. If it's thought about as permanent, unchangeable, and pervasive, that's pessimism.*

10. ***Optimists are an active bunch, and activity seems to keep us healthier.*** "Here's the really important piece to understand," says Suzanne Segerstrom, a University of Kentucky psychologist and author of *Breaking Murphy's Law: How Optimists Get What They Want from Life—and Pessimists Can Too*. "If you're an optimist and working harder at a task, your stress hormones may go up. Your immune function may dip a bit. But it's like doing crunches at the gym. Short-term, more crunches hurt. Long-term, you get a big payback in terms of health and fitness. Optimism leads to increased well-being because it leads you to engage actively in life, not because of a miracle happy juice that optimists have and pessimists don't."[8]

11. *Reframe life circumstances to find new meaning.* This ability is part of an optimist's world view. Optimists make more life-affirming choices in the midst of disappointments, challenges, and lost opportunities. "When a crisis strikes," says University of Virginia psychologist Jonathan Haidt, author of *The Happiness Hypothesis*, "optimists tend to alternate between active coping and reappraisal. If active coping fails to fix the problem, they reappraise the situation, looking for hidden benefits, and, invested with flexibility, write a new chapter for their life."[9] For Extraordinary Leaders, this means reframing a failed project, negative employee experience, or bad decision into a learning oportunity. Your ability to train your people to do this kind of reframing will allow them to make mistakes without fear of being humiliated.

12. **Don't hesitate to kick pessimism to the curb every chance you get.** As I've mentioned before, we humans have what psychologists call a negativity bias. It's our nature to fixate on bad news, to forecast doom and gloom. This built-in paranoia is a holdover from our hunter-gatherer days, when survival meant constantly looking out for danger. "The same neuro-hormonal chemistry that evolved to get us away from charging lions is locked and loaded today when we feel the least bit threatened," says Rick Hanson, PhD, founder of the Wellspring Institute for Neuroscience and Contemplative Wisdom. But while this bias for "fight or flight" *(and I'd add freeze)* may have been helpful in the Serengeti, its over-use these days is detrimental to our health and well-being, not to mention any accomplishments we might make.[10]

It seems that optimism is the digitalis of pessimism. It brings us back to life. It rights our ship, so to speak. Susan Vaughan, MD, author of *Half Empty, Half Full: How to Take Control and Live*

Life as an Optimist, agrees. She describes optimistic behavior as a psychological righting reflex. "It's like cats," she says. "When you throw them out the window, they always land on their feet." If you know perennial optimists, I'll bet you'll agree that describes their landing on their feet ability.[11]

> **Putting It Into Practice:**
>
> Play the "Reframe Game." When you realize you are in a negative or depressed mood, imagine you are holding a clapboard. Snap your hands together and say, out loud, "Take 2!" Then consciously choose to look at your situation from a more optimistic perspective.
>
> (If it doesn't work the first time, you can always "Take 3, Take 4, ... Take as many as you need—just like in the movies!"

This next point is REALLY important! Having an Optimistic Spirit does not mean you are viewing the world through rose-colored glasses, ignoring the challenges and pain you experience. *(Feel free to read that last statement again. I'll wait!)* The difference lies in the way you deal wtih those situations. People with an optimistic spirit know how to bounce back after setbacks. Martin Seligman, Ph.D. (remember him? I gave you his credentials earlier in this chapter) wrote a great book entitled *Learned Optimism: How to Change Your Mind and Your Life.* In it, he shares an ABCD Model he calls *Learned Optimism*[12] as an approach to reduce our negativity and pessimism and strengthen this Core Ability of Optimistic Spirit. It works like this:

> **A = Adversity:** Be aware of what you say to yourself about the obstacles, failures, and adverse events that occur in your life.
>
> **B = Belief:** Note your beliefs about the event that has occurred. How do you perceive yourself?
>
> **C = Consequences:** Be aware of the consequences in the moment and the impact that this will have in the future. How do you feel about this event? How will this impact you in the future?
>
> **D = Distract or Dispute**: Distract yourself if it is a minor event; if the event is more serious, dispute it by identifying the actual facts supporting it; assessing alternative responses to the event and the implications of each response; and questioning the usefulness of the beliefs you have about the event.

The very process of using this ABCD approach allows you to make the conscious decision to tap into your Core Ability of Optimistic Spirit, which opens your mind to potential solutions.

It might help to see the ABCD process in a practical example for leaders. Suppose one of your employees made a major error that resulted in you receiving a chewing out from your boss. You are irritated with the employee, embarrassed to be belittled by your boss, and stressed out about what to do next. Remembering the ABCD Model, you call on your Core Ability of Optimistic Spirit to put it into practice. It might look something like this:

A=Adversity: Your employee's mistake, the subsequent dressing down by your boss, the impact on your team and yourself, and your decision about what to do next are all factors impacting this event that is causing you distress.

B=Belief: You realize you are feeling extremely inadequate as a leader. How else could you have an employee who would make such a disastrous mistake? Why else would your manager yell at you? You are festering a belief in your own inability to be an effective leader, and are questioning your role in the company.

C= Consequences: Your team is feeling defeated; the employee who made the mistake is fearing for his job; you are wondering if you have any credibility left with your manager. Continuing with this way of thinking will result in decreased engagement and morale in your team, and possibly loss of personnel. It could also lead to a declining relationship with your manager, and a decrease in your impact with the executive team as a whole.

D= Distract or Dispute: Since this is a pretty major situation, it's time to practice "Dispute." You can start by questioning the usefulness of your beliefs around this issue. You realize you have worked hard to create an environment where employees are empowered to be creative and take initiative. This individual is normally an outstanding performer, who just made a poor choice with this particular project. You have received many kudos from your manager in the past, and are a respected member of the executive team. These facts help you put this situation into perspective, and allow you to focus your energy and attention on how to move forward in a way that will maintain the level of engagement and initiative your team possesses, and allow everyone to grow from the experience.

Obviously, this is a capsulized version of how the model works, and there is a lot of detail missing. But hopefully it gives you an idea of how practical it can be in helping you transform your thinking into a useful, productive mode.

You may be asking, does this Core Ability of Optimisitc Spirit have any usefulness for leaders in the C-Suite, (CEOs, CFOs, COOs, etc.). Again turning to research, Jeffrey E. Garten, dean of the Yale School of Management, interviewed 40 of the world's most successful C-Suite business executives for his book, *The Mind of the CEO*. Garten found every last one of them to be extremely optimistic. "I didn't find a lot of other common traits," he says. "For example, conventional wisdom says these are all alpha people who exude aggressiveness and do nothing in life besides work. I didn't find that. But the one thing they had in common was how they all talked about the mountains they had to climb every single day." CEOs, it

Optimistic Spirit

seems, keep a perspective on the tasks at hand by placing them within a larger, more strategic vision. "Their view was," Garten asserts, "I know I have succeeded in the past, and I'm quite confident that if I can look beyond today's problems to a point on the horizon, I know I'm going to get there."

A key component in their optimism seems to be an absolute willingness to look for the bright side, no matter what happens. They also used self-talk to combat negative internal messages as if they were debating an external foe. When you conquer pessimism head-on, your chances of achieving your objectives are doubled, and even tripled.[13]

An optimistic spirit is a beautiful state of mind. I believe an optimistic spirit, not the negativity bias, is hardwired into our brain, and as a result, we are all endowed with an Extraordinary Nature which is characterized by all of the qualities we need to make our human experience worthwhile, happy, healthy, and productive. An Optimistic Spirit is one of the chief qualities of our extraordinariness, and an incredibly powerful tool for the Extraordinary Leader.

The Ability & the Color: Summary

Optimistic Spirit: Maintaining a positive outlook regardless of the appearances. With an Optimistic Spirit, you are able to move beyond failures, disappointments, negative experiences, or difficult situations, because you hold a world view that recognizes the innate good that exists within every opportunity.

The Color Orange: Orange is the color of warmth, happiness, and optimism. It is a color which keeps us motivated and focused on the positive aspects of life. Orange is the color of Optimistic Spirit because when you operate from a belief in the positive side of life, you can overcome negativity and disappointment, knowing you are being true to the Extraordinary You!

Cultivating Your Optimistic Spirit

Optimism is essential to achievement and it is also the foundation of courage and true progress.
(Nicholas M. Butler)

Laser Focus Technique:

Preparation:

> Prepare for this Laser Focus experience by finding a quiet location where you will be uninterrupted. Sit in a comfortable position that you can hold for 20-25 minutes.
>
> Take a few deep breaths, exhaling slowly between each breath. Without trying to force your breath in any way, allow it to find its own natural depth and rhythm. Always breathe through your nose. (That's assuming your nasal passages are clear and unobstructed. Otherwise breathe through your mouth.)
>
> Allow your attention to focus either on the sensation of your breath coming and going through your nostrils, or on the rising and falling of your belly as you breathe.
>
> Give your full attention to the coming and going of your breath.
>
> If you realize your attention has wandered, and you find yourself engrossed in thinking ahead or day-dreaming, simply acknowledge the ego's trespass, then gently bring your attention back to your breathing.

The Process:

> Think about a positive work-related experience you had this week. (If you have difficulty identifying something, think further back until an experience comes into your awareness.)

In your mind's eye recapture the experience. Be as specific as you can.

Were you alone or with others? If you were with others, who was involved in this experience? Was your experience the result of something planned or spontaneous? What sounds are you hearing? What emotions are being expressed? Where is the experience happening? Relive the moment as vividly as possible, knowing it is simply a recollection of the prior event itself.

To what extent does the fond memory feed your optimism? How does it affect your present mood? Do you have a sense that you'd like more upbeat, cheerful, hopeful moments to define your work as a leader on a regular basis?

Now, let's add a positive experience that hasn't happened yet. Think of a future work-related moment that you would like to experience as an upbeat, exhilarating, inspiring experience. Remember, it's something that hasn't happened yet, but is possibly scheduled or anticipated. It could even be an upbeat event that you wish you could experience. Whatever the expectation, visualize the experience as vividly and optimistically as you can. Be as specific and descriptive as possible. Stretch yourself to be even more optimistically positive than you might think possible.

As you bring this optimistic adventure to a close, think how wonderful it would be to fill your life with optimistic adventures everyday. Suppose you were the kind of leader who was upbeat no matter what life throws at you? Consider that last question for the next few moments as you pay attention to your breathing. Make sure you are breathing normally and rhythmically.

Realize that having an Optimistic Spirit is one of your Core Abilities. Rest assured that optimism is a quality you possess. It's in your DNA. So, take a few moments to think to yourself: *I am the kind of leader who remains optimistic no matter what life throws at me.* Repeat that personal description at least five times.

Now, think: *I expect my desire for positive outcomes to define my leadership style.* Repeat that positive statement at least five times.

Take a few moments to consider what that means. If positive outcomes define your leadership style, how would you treat your employees? What would your work experience be like? How confident would you be? How would you handle problems? What would you do differently than you are doing right now? Who would you keep in your sphere of influence?

Spend some quality time on each of these questions before you bring this Laser Focus session to a close.

When you feel you are going to end this Laser Focus experience on an optimistic note, conclude the session by taking a slow deep breath and saying out loud, "I am an optimistic leader. I claim my Optimistic Spirit right here, right now!" Repeat those statements aloud five times.

Self-Directed Activity to Develop Your Optimistic Spirit Core Ability: Be a Can Guru

There are so many leaders who are ready to tell their employees why they can't do something, and there are so many opportunities to be involved with spreading bad news. This activity casts you in the important role of the Can Guru!

For the next seven days, do everything you can to play the role of Can Guru. Here are some things to add to your repertoire:

Start with yourself. When your Inner Critic begins to tell you that you cannot do something, simply direct it to off stage. Reinforce your role by repeating your lines over and over: *I am a Can Guru. Oh, yes I can!*

Change the conversation. When you find yourself in a group, and the conversation becomes negative, jump in as a Can Guru. This does not mean you refuse to see the negative things that are happening. Instead, you become a leader who chooses to focus on how to use it for good. (For example, if people are moaning about the lack of resources available for a project, focus on identifying creative, unique ways to use resources already accessible.)

Reframe the news. No matter how terrible the news is, look for ways to reframe it to focus on the positive. If there has been a horrible setback, comment on the brilliant way individuals were able to handle the situation quickly. If you need to communicate a difficult decision, include the positive impact it will have, and how you plan to help your team cope with the news.

Support other people in their dreams. Provide support for the goals of others, and look for ways to help them achieve their dreams. Offer positive encouragement; recommend resources; share your own experiences; be their cheerleader. Sometimes your positive support can be the tipping point in another person's ability to succeed.

Monitor your activities ... and the impact they have on you. At the end of each day, spend time reflecting back over the day. Identify every Can Guru activity you performed, and jot it in your journal. As you look back over the list, capture your feelings about what you've done. How has it changed the way you see things?

How has it impacted your relationships? In what ways are you a different person as a result of your focus?

You might even want to adopt the kangaroo (can-guru) as your new mascot, symbolizing your ability to jump in to claim the optimistic viewpoint and positive attitude in every situation!

Using the Color Orange:

If you want to strengthen your awareness of your Optimistic Spirit, make Orange your color of focus. Choose to wear something orange as part of your wardrobe; eat foods that are orange in color (oranges, sweet potatoes, carrots, cheddar cheese, Doritos, pumpkin, cantaloupe, peaches etc.); place items that are orange in your environment (orange flowers, an orange stone, pictures with orange as a dominant color). You may even want to use orange ink or markers when you write.

While this may feel a little silly at first, allow yourself to give it a try without judgment. Become aware of how much more positive you feel, how you are focusing in ways to use everything for good, and how you are experiencing the Optimistic Spirit in your life and in your leadership style.

Personal Reflections

*Date:*_____

Chapter 6: Self-Reliance

People with a strong [Self-Reliant perspective] believe that the responsibility for whether or not they get reinforced ultimately lies with themselves. Internals believe that success or failure is due to their own efforts. In contrast, externals believe that the reinforcers in life are controlled by luck, chance, or powerful others. Therefore, they see little impact of their own efforts on the amount of reinforcement they receive. (Julian Rotter)

Guess what's been reported to be the number one contributor to happiness and success? Money? No. Good looks? Nope. Popularity? Not even close. Power? Guess again!

According to a report by *The Journal of Personality and Social Psychology,* all these mentioned 'happiness guarantors' were topped by the biggest guarantor of them all: 'autonomy, defined as 'the feeling that your life, with all its activities and habits, is self-chosen and self-endorsed.' Knowing you possess that kind of autonomy is called Self-Reliance. Americans consider autonomy more important to them than power, moral goodness, and even winning the lottery.[1]

Self-Reliance is a concept that personality psychology calls "Internal Locus of Control." It refers to the extent to which people believe they can control events that affect their lives. Originally developed by Julian B. Rotter in 1954, it has since become a key concept in social-learning theory. A person's center (locus) is characterized as either internal (the person believes they are self-reliant, that they can control their life) or external (meaning they believe that their decisions and experiences in life are controlled by outside factors which they cannot influence). In Extraordinary Leadership, this Core Ability of Self-Reliance is critical.

If you operate from a Self-Reliant perspective as a leader, you lead from the knowledge that you're in charge of your results. If you succeed, you believe your skills, talents, and abilities had a great deal to do with it—and if you fail, you take personal responsibility.

Leaders with high Self-Reliance believe that events in their life derive primarily from their own actions. On the other hand, leaders with an external center of control (victim perspective) believe other people, the environment, outer circumstances, or some higher power controls what happens. Essentially, these individuals feel dependent on something outside of themselves or even helpless at times. That means it's easy to point the finger at everyone and everything but themselves; hence the label victim perspective. Leaders with this perspective create chaos on their teams, because they never take responsibility for problems. People walk on egg shells around them for fear of being the brunt of their tirades.

Because the focus of control is the key for this Core Ability, we could call those who exhibit high Self-Reliance *Internals*; those with a Victim Perspective could be called *Externals*. [2] These characteristics apply to your employees as well, and understanding this can help you lead more effectively. (I affectionately nickname these descriptors as "Innies" and "Outies.")

For example, team members with high Self-Reliance (Innies) who do not perform as well as they wanted to on a project would blame it on lack of preparedness or skill on their part. If these same team members performed well on a project, they would attribute this to their ability to prepare and use their strengths as required for the project. Conversely, if team members with a high victim perspective (Outies) perform poorly on a project, they might attribute this to the difficulty of the project or inability of other team members to carry their weight. If they performed well on a project, they might think the leader was lenient or that they were lucky.

Self-Reliance

Innies tend to attribute outcomes of events to their own control. People who have high Self-Reliance believe that their hard work leads them to obtain positive outcomes. They also believe that every action has its consequence, which makes them accept the fact that things happen and it depends on them whether they want to have control over it or not.

Outies typically attribute outcomes of events to external circumstances. People who have an external center of control believe that many things that happen in their lives are out of their control, and they tend to point fingers, make excuses, and place blame rather than work to resolve issues.[3]

How does this apply to you as a leader? Reflect on how you have personally handled disappointments, frustrations, victories, and achievements in your life. For example, if your team is involved in a major project at work that does not go as well as you'd hoped, do you find yourself blaming specific team members, lack of information, or unavailable resources from your manager (outie)? Or are you willing to look at what can be learned from the situation, and recognize your ineffectiveness at clarifying the expectations up front, asking the right questions, negotiating for resources, or selecting the right people for the team (innie)?

If you receive an unexpected award, do you consider it luck (outie), or do you acknowledge your hard work to earn the recognition (innie)?

> Studies link Self-Reliance with improved physical health, mental health, and quality of life in people with diverse conditions: HIV, migraines, diabetes, kidney disease and epilepsy.[4]

What Does Science Say?

Obviously, most of us don't operate with a locus of control that's completely internal or external. But generally, we're more on the scale towards one or the other—and each has its own set of outcomes.

> *Having a strong sense of controlling one's life is a more dependable predictor of positive feelings of well-being than any of the objective conditions of life we have considered.*
>
> *(Angus Campbell, researcher)*

A University of Michigan nationwide survey sings the praises of a Self-Reliant perspective—reporting how the 15% of Americans who claim they feel "in control of their lives" also rave about having "extraordinarily positive feelings of happiness."

The survey recommends that if an obnoxious life challenge is making you feel out of control, stop lying around doing nothing. Stop telling and re-telling your story. Stop sleeping late. Stop watching too much TV. Stop postponing things you enjoy. Start recognizing that giving power to outer appearances will only increase your feelings of being out of control and victimized.[5]

Can you see the correlation with your actions as a leader? I've worked with far too many people holding leadership titles and control over others who were deeply rooted in external, victim perspectives. Their behaviors at work are characterized by unpredictable rants, time in the break room drinking too much coffee and eating too many doughnuts, complaining about their higher-ups and blaming their employees for poor performance. The result: a totally disengaged workforce who follow the lead and pattern their behaviors after their manager.

Self-Reliance

What's interesting is that Portland State University educator, Dr. Al Siebert, author of *The Resiliency Advantage and Survivor Personality*, argued that "both sets of these beliefs can be self-validating and self-fulfilling. People who believe that their fate is under the control of outside forces act in ways that confirm their beliefs. People who know they can do things to make their lives better act in ways to confirm their beliefs. The question we must ask ourselves is: How do we want to live—as a victim or as a victor?"[6]

Check Yourself Out: Are You an "Innie" or an "Outie?"

Being in control is a choice. And leaders who have gotten in touch with their Extraordinary Nature have chosen to endorse their own abilities, talents, and skills as the reason they are successful and happy. As the environment around you changes, you can either attribute your success and failure to things you have control over, or assign the blame or credit to forces outside your influence. Which orientation you choose—whether you're an "innie" or an "outie"—has a direct bearing on your long-term success and happiness as a leader (and for that matter, as a person). Check out the descriptors that follow by marking the boxes listing behaviors that describe you a majority of the time. Add them up, and determine whether you are more of an "innie" or an "outie."

> If you are an 'outie' (primarily operate from a Victim Perspective), you're more likely to:
> - ❏ Believe luck, chance, and/or fate decides what happens to you.
> - ❏ Be habitually negative and give up more easily when setbacks occur.
> - ❏ Fail to create new relationships or try to repair old ones.
> - ❏ Feel more helpless when faced with stress or illness.
> - ❏ Wear your victim status like a badge of honor.
> - ❏ Blame everyone and everything but yourself.
> - ❏ Want to be led by others.
> - ❏ Avoid tough responsibilities at all costs.
> - ❏ Are more prone to stress, anxiety, and depression.

> If you are an 'innie' (primarily operate from a Self-Reliant perspective), you're more likely to:
> - ❑ Think you're responsible for your success and failure.
> - ❑ Be less prone to chronic anxiety and depression.
> - ❑ Be more independent and achievement-oriented.
> - ❑ Be more health-conscious and disciplined in lifestyle changes related to improved health and well-being.
> - ❑ Feel confident that you can be successful.
> - ❑ Prefer leading rather than following.
> - ❑ Exhibit greater control over your behavior and actions.
> - ❑ Seek to learn as much as you can.
> - ❑ Deal with life-threatening challenges and extreme stress better.
> - ❑ Use challenges to come out stronger than before.
> - ❑ Thrive in the midst of unplanned change.
> - ❑ Are less likely to mindlessly submit to authority.

Few would discount the importance of cultivating a Self-Reliant perspective. The important question to ask is what can be done to change one's center of control orientation, to practice a higher level of Self-Reliance? In the continuous improvement mindset of author and consultant W. Edwards Deming, even the best practices and processes can be improved and honed. I agree! Are you ready to dig in and strengthen your Self-Reliance as a leader?

Strengthening Your Core Ability of Self-Reliance

If your center of control isn't as 'internal' as you'd like it to be, there are things you can do right now to cultivate your center of control to an internal orientation and empower yourself. Here are a few ideas to get you started:

1. ***Notice your language and self-talk.*** If you tend to speak in absolutes (ie., using words like always, never, everyone, no one), stop. Be more specific and realistic in your terminology. If your self-talk is generally negative, work on getting out of your negativity bias and choose to see yourself (and others) in a more positive light.

2. ***Phase out attitudes like, 'I have no choice' and 'I can't do this or that.'*** You can replace them with, 'I choose not to,' or, 'Next time I will handle it differently.' Realizing and acknowledging that you always have a choice (even if the choices you have aren't ideal) can help you change your situation, or accept it more easily if it really is the best of all available options.

3. ***Monitor what you think, say, and do.*** Your attitude affects your stress level and health more than you may realize. Become aware of what you are thinking, saying, and doing, and make intentional changes toward a more healthy positivity bias.

4. ***Begin to take personal responsibility instead of blaming others.*** Self-Reliance develops slowly throughout the life span, and takes conscious effort and awareness to strengthen. Many people are not even aware that they blame others for their own shortcomings or errors and see the world as a controlling force that dictates their lives and happiness. Start paying attention to where you are placing blame and responsibility.

5. ***Take the words 'luck' and 'fate' out of your vocabulary.*** You are in control of your destiny. Focus on the things you can control that will increase productivity and work culture.

6. ***Reflect on the things you may have presumed you have no control over.*** Think carefully about whether your assumptions are accurate. Certain events and people may have upset and/or disappointed you, but you always have control over how you respond to them now.

7. ***Once you have accepted that you always have choices, the next step is to take the situations where you feel trapped and brainstorm alternatives.*** This will both solidify the belief that you have choices as well as help you maintain the realism you need to feel in control.

8. ***Claim your 'Internal' Status as a leader.*** 'Innies' take action, claim responsibility, and initiate results, while 'outies' believe things are done to them. Seeing things outside

of you as the cause of your successes or failures is a recipe for chronic unhappiness, indecision, and depression—not to mention a disengaged workforce with low productivity and morale.

> **Putting It Into Practice:**
> Play the game of "Gotcha!" Begin paying attention to the words you say and the thoughts you have. Whenever you hear yourself saying or thinking anything that indicates a belief in an external center of control, immediately say (out loud, if possible) "Gotcha!" Once you catch yourself, then replace the phrase with one that claims Self-Reliance. Notice how quickly you begin to change your focus!

The reason Self-Reliance is such an important Core Ability of an Extraordinary Leader is because, while every action has its consequence, a particular action is the result of a personal choice that caused that effect (consequence). Success and happiness in leadership and in fact, in life, come as we accept the fact that while "things" happen, it is our choice to have control over them or not. The one thing we always control is our reaction to whatever occurs.

Self-Reliance

When you have a strong Self-Reliance, you harness inner resolve that helps you rebound from a setback or challenge, such as a job loss, an illness, a disaster, or the death of a loved one. If you lack a strong Self-Reliant perspective, you might dwell on problems, feel victimized, become overwhelmed, or turn to unhealthy coping mechanisms, such as substance abuse. A Self-Reliant perspective won't make your problems go away—but it can give you the ability to see past them, better handle stress, and be a more effective leader. Self-Reliance is the ability to roll with the punches. When stress, adversity, or trauma strikes, you still experience anger, grief, and pain, but you're able to keep functioning—both physically and psychologically.[7]

This Core Ability, like each of the other Core Abilities, is a necessary condition for accessing your Authentic Self, the Extraordinary You, your Core Nature ... so you can be an Extraordinary Leader.

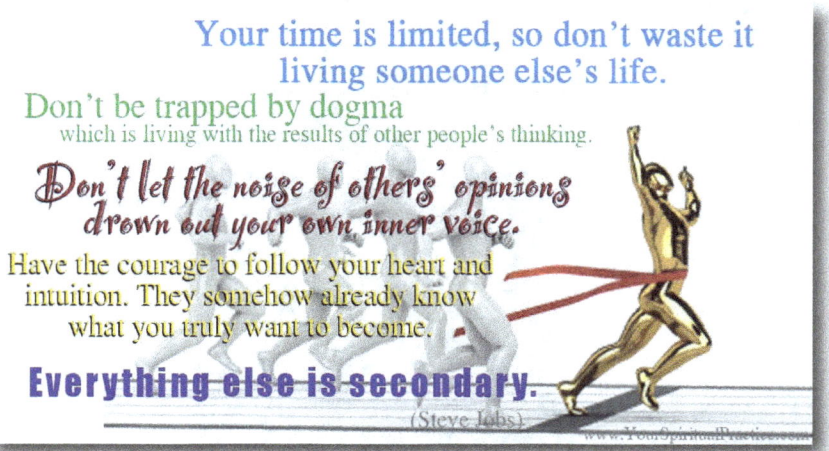

Your time is limited, so don't waste it living someone else's life. Don't be trapped by dogma which is living with the results of other people's thinking. Don't let the noise of others' opinions drown out your own inner voice. Have the courage to follow your heart and intuition. They somehow already know what you truly want to become. Everything else is secondary.
(Steve Jobs)

The Ability & the Color: Summary

Self-Reliance: The recognition that you control your fate, rather than relying on outer circumstances, people, or luck. The power of choice plays a key role in activating your Self-Reliance, and as an Extraordinary Leader it allows you to take charge, regardless of the situation. When you operate from the Self-Reliant perspective, you are a victor rather than a victim.

The Color Purple: Purple is the color of depth of understanding and transformation. It represents Self-Reliance because it signifies your ability to transform any life situation or circumstance through your power of choice. It represents your ability as a leader to claim responsibility for your results, knowing you are leading from the Extraordinary You!

Cultivating Your Self-Reliance

You are everything you choose to be. You are as unlimited as the endless universe. (Shad Helmstetter)

Laser Focus Technique:

Preparation:

Prepare for this Laser Focus experience by finding a quiet location where you will be uninterrupted. Sit in a comfortable position that you can hold for 20-25 minutes.

Take a few deep breaths, exhaling slowly between each breath. Without trying to force your breath in any way, allow it to find its own natural depth and rhythm. Always breathe through your nose. (That's assuming your nasal passages are clear and unobstructed. Otherwise breathe through your mouth.)

Allow your attention to focus either on the sensation of your breath coming and going through your nostrils, or on the rising and falling of your belly as you breathe.

Give your full attention to the coming and going of your breath.

If you realize your attention has wandered, and you find yourself engrossed in thinking ahead or day-dreaming, simply acknowledge the ego's trespass, then gently but firmly bring your attention back to your breathing.

The Process:

Take just a few moments to think about what the power of choice means. Do you believe you always have a choice, or do you believe there are times when you have no choice? Do you see yourself as acting or reacting in the face of challenges? Are you victor or victim? Do you draw on your inner resources or wait for outer events to determine your direction?

Pay attention to your self-talk. When you hear yourself thinking things like, "I have no choice" or "There's nothing I can do," sit back and remind yourself that you do, in fact, have more control than you might think.

Spend as much quality time on these questions as you feel you need to. When you are satisfied with your reasoning take a few slow, deep breaths as closure.

Think to yourself: *My actions are always the result of my thoughts, intentions, and choices*. Mentally repeat that positive self talk statement to yourself until it feels comfortable to think that about yourself.

Pay attention to your breathing. Make sure you are breathing normally and rhythmically. Repeat that same positive, self-defining statement aloud: *My actions are always the result of my thoughts, intentions, and choices*. Repeat the statement aloud at least five times in succession confidently and resolutely.

Realize that you always have a choice to change your situation. Even if you don't like the choices available at the moment, even if the only choice you can make is to change your attitude, you always have a choice. Say to yourself out loud: *I always have a choice*. Repeat that positive, life-affirming statement at least ten times.

Become aware of your breathing. With every inhalation, think: *I am a choice master;* and with every exhalation, think: *I use my power to choose*. Repeat this series of thoughtful inhalations and exhalations for several minutes.

Take the next few minutes to assure yourself that you are the 'captain of your consciousness.' Say to yourself: *I am the captain of my consciousness*. Reposition yourself by sitting up a little straighter as you affirm your captaincy.

Self-Reliance

Below is a random list of positive self talk statements that are self-reliance-building words or phrases. All of them emphasize your Self-Reliance. Choose three to focus on during the next few minutes. Choose only three now, and then the next time you use this technique, you can select three different ones. Here are the statements and words/phrases (feel free to add your own):

- I am the one who attaches meaning to what happens.
- I am a problem-solver.
- I welcome change and ambiguity.
- I see failures and mistakes as learning opportunities.
- I have high self-esteem.
- I am achievement-oriented.
- I control my own destiny.
- I am a calculated risk-taker.
- I have the wherewithal to do anything.
- I am self-actualized.
- I am goal-oriented.
- I have personal power.
- I optimize performance excellence as a leader.
- I am success-oriented.
- I have the right amount of determination.
- I am resourceful.
- I am an Extraordinary Leader.

In your mind's eye see yourself handling a life situation coming up. It can be from your personal life or from your professional life. Use the words and/or positive self-talk statements you chose above to frame your responses to the life situation you have chosen. See yourself successfully handling the situation from a Self-Reliant perspective. Employ these words/phrases to your advantage and for the benefit of all concerned in your mental scenario.

Spend whatever time you need to fully develop the above scene. Employ the Self-Reliance characteristics to guarantee its success.

As your scenario comes to a close, direct your attention to your breathing. Focus on the length and quality of your breathing. If you need to slow your breathing take a few moments now to do so, making sure your breaths are normal and rhythmical.

Remind yourself that like any other skill or personal trait development, the more you practice the better at it you get. You can develop this core essence with practice and determination. It is one of the seven Core Abilities associated with the Extraordinary You. So the more you use it, the more connected you will become with yourself as an Extraordinary Leader.

Self-Directed Activity to Develop Your Self-Reliance Core Ability: Exercise Your Power of Choice

This is a great activity to remind yourself how much power you have in any situation. Here's how it works:

When you realize you are in a situation where you feel frustrated, stuck, overwhelmed, or stymied, use the following process to tap into your Self-Reliance by exercising your power of choice:

> Step 1—Ask yourself: *Do I have a choice?* (By the way, the answer to this one is almost always yes. Of course, we may not always like our choices, but we ultimately get to choose how we respond in any situation!)
>
> Step 2—Ask yourself: *What are the choices I can make?* (This is a really important step, because it allows you to specifically recognize your choices and determine the potential consequences of each one.)
>
> Step 3—Make a choice: Claim your power by completing the following statement: *I choose to (fill in the action you have chosen) because (fill in the reason you believe it is the best choice in this situation).*

Here's a simple example to illustrate the power of this activity. Imagine you have an employee named Bob who is creating problems on the team. You know you need to have a discussion with Bob, but you don't really want to because you dread the emotional fallout. It feels easier to just ignore the problem. But as his manager, you know it is your responsibility to deal with the issue. Once you realize you are struggling over the decision of whether or not to confront Bob, ask the questions:

- Do I have a choice? *Yes, I do!*
- What are the choices I can make? *I can choose to schedule the meeting with Bob so I can get it over with and move on. Or I can ignore the problem and focus on*

other things, but then this guy will only get worse—and it will affect my other employees. Or I could pass it off to my supervisor ... but then I would feel like an incompetent leader who can't handle my team effectively.

- Make a choice: *I choose to schedule the meeting with Bob immediately so I can get it over with. I will write up a a detailed outline so I feel prepared when I talk with him, and include actual action items for future expectations and consequences.*

Here's the deal: Even though the ultimate end result is still holding the meeting you were dreading, you now feel better about it and more in control, because you *chose* to do it rather than feeling *forced* to do it. That reinforces your Self-Reliance.

Using the Color Purple:

If you want to strengthen your awareness of your Self-Reliance, make purple your color of focus. Choose to wear something purple as part of your wardrobe; eat foods that are purple in color (grapes, egg plant. purple cabbage, beets, plums, etc.); place items that are purple in your environment (purple flowers, a purple stone, pictures with purple as a dominant color). Use purple ink or markers when you write.

While this may feel a little silly at first, allow yourself to give it a try without judgment. Become aware of how much more in control you feel, how your choices are more powerful and self-affirming, and how you are experiencing Self-Reliance as an Extraordinary Leader.

Personal Reflections

Date:_____

Chapter 7: Mentoring Mindset

*Mentoring is a brain to pick, an ear to listen, and
a push in the right direction.
(John Crosby)*

When you hear the term "Mentor," most folks automatically think of formal programs designed to link a seasoned expert with a protogé, to guide the individual along their chosen career path. They typically envision an assigned relationship over a specifed period of time, with structured processes in place to identify goals and measure progress.

While this type of formal mentoring program is beneficial and powerful, embraced by over 70% of Fortune 500 companies, it is only one type of mentoring. I have something very different in mind when I refer to the Core Ability of a Mentoring Mindset.

Let's jump into this discussion by tossing two questions at you as attention getters:

- On a scale of 1 to 10, with 10 being highest, where would you place yourself in terms of how rich you are?
- On a scale of 1 to 10, with 10 being highest, where would you place yourself in terms of how much you give?

I hope these opening questions gave you a moment of pause, because they are central to the essence of a Mentoring Mindset. Okay, I'll admit that these were kind of trick questions! As you look at the rankings you gave yourself, consider this: were you thinking only in terms of money? If so, consider what other things could be included in your assessment. As a leader, you are rich in terms of the enormous amount of wisdom, insight, experiences, knowledge, and skill—not to mention connections and relationships—just waiting to be passed on to others. It does not require a formal, structured program for you to do this. Instead, it is a way of operating as an Extraordinary Leader. That is the essence of a Mentoring Mindset.

A Mentoring Mindset refers to a way of seeing every situation as a learning opportunity; of always being in touch with what your people are doing, so you can casually or intentionally provide guidance, wisdom, skills, recommendations, and resources to grow the professional maturity and ability of all your people.

Leaders who use a Mentoring Mindset are able to work with their people to ensure:

- Project successes can be replicated by helping people identify the contributing behaviors and actions that led to the success;
- Project failures can be transformed into learning laboratories, to avoid the same pitfalls on future projects;
- Fears can be overcome through understanding, skill building, practice, and feedback;
- Employees can embrace empowerment by learning how to think strategically, apply policies, make wise decisions, and use resources effectively.

Mentoring Reduces Stress

Lebena Varghese and three colleagues at Northern Illinois University conducted a study that found mentoring is effective for individuals vulnerable to severe stress because they don't feel capable of handling the job responsibilities for which they are held accountable, or because they find their work environment overwhelming.[5]

Extraordinary Leaders who manage from a Mentoring Mindset are sensitive to the signs of stress and burnout in their people, and can provide critical support, a listening ear, and well-timed strategic interventions to alleviate the stress.

Leaders employing a Mentoring Mindset do not wait until performance appraisal time to correct someone who is off-course; instead, coaching and mentoring become a day-to-day routine part of the job. As an Extraordinary Leader, you are always on the lookout for ways to share insights, offer guidance in decision making and problem solving, model behaviors you want to see manifested, and encourage employees to stretch themselves. The benefits will flow back in a multitude of ways: enhanced engagement, increased initiative and creativity, improved relationships among team members, more powerful bottom-line results—just to name a few!

What Does Science Say?

There are a number of scientific findings that reinforce the value of a Mentoring Mindset. Neuro-biologically speaking, a Mentoring Mindset falls into the realm of helpfulness and generosity, nestled within the same frontal regions of the brain that are activated by awe, wonder, transcendence, and joy. An internal coherence results, which fortifies your immune system, strengthens the neural pathways in the frontal lobe, and arrests the feelings of fear and uncertainty, which are the products of the amygdala.[1]

> Generosity and helpfulness for many are driven by a sincere desire to benefit others. If you're helpful, you receive more respect, you have more influence and people cooperate with you more.[2]

In another study, organizational psychologist Adam Grant identified three types of attitudes encountered in the workplace: *Givers; Takers;* and *Matchers*. Givers epitomize helpfulness and generosity, expressing the Mentoring Mindset of giving by such acts as being open with information, making time to assist others in their projects, and giving credit to others for ideas and work. Takers, on the other hand, are basically looking out for themselves, asking for help but rarely offering it. Matchers live in a reciprocal mindset of trading favors, recognition, and assistance in a "you scratch my back and I'll scratch yours" mindset.

According to this research, Givers experienced more meaning in their work, were more resilient, and handled stressful events more effectively than Takers or Matchers.[3]

> Performing generous acts (through mentoring) makes both the giver and the receiver feel more valued and appreciated. This spills over into numerous successful life outcomes, including superior physical and mental health, enhanced creativity and productivity, higher income, more prosocial behavior, and stronger interpersonal relationships.[4]

Research at the University of California in San Diego and Harvard University (posted in an online edition of the *Proceedings of the National Academy of Sciences*) provides laboratory evidence that helpful behavior spreads between people. Those who benefit from a generous act tend to find it contagious—and "pay it forward" by helping others. James Fowler, an associate professor of political science at UC San Diego, and Nicholas Christakis, a

Harvard sociology professor, showed that when one person gave money in a "public-goods game" to help others, the recipients were more likely to give money away in the future. The *domino effect* continued as more people were swept up in the tide of kindness and cooperation, according to the researchers. In short, Fowler said: "You don't go back to being your 'old selfish self.'" [5]

This *domino effect* occurs in the workplace as well. When you lead with a visible desire to offer guidance, and turn mistakes into learning opportunities, you will see your people demonstrating the same behaviors as they work with others. By strengthening your Mentoring Mindset, you are in a position to create a workplace more conducive to engagement, better able to serve customers heroically, and ignite creativity and teamwork at the highest possible levels.

Putting It Into Practice:

Brainstorm a list of ways you can mentor your employees informally. See if you can stretch yourself to come up with at least 12.

1.
2.
3.
4.
5.
6.
7.
8.
9.
10.
11.
12.

Leaders often ask me why they should even *want* to strengthen this Core Ability. Because I am so incredibly passionate about this particular Core Ability, let me make a case for it before providing ways to strengthen it. Leaders who operate from a Mentoring Mindset develop a culture rich with engagement among their employees. Why is this important? According to one study, conducted by Blessing/White, actively engaged employees come to the workplace with a desire to give. They work with passion and feel a profound connection to their company. 88% of highly engaged employees believe they can positively impact the quality of their organization's products, compared with only 38% of those who are disengaged.[6]

This attitude leads to increased sharing of information between departments, more camaraderie among employees, and a focus on the customer that creates a positive experience, leading to repeat and referral business. The culture is one of a learning organization, with formal and informal mentoring taking place, not just between the leader and team, but also among team members. In addition, companies that foster a Mentoring Mindset are able to integrate new employees onto the team more quickly. They also tend to be more active in finding opportunities to openly communicate with other departments within the organization, and actively participate in giving back to their communities and favorite charities. Everyone wins when there is a Mentoring Mindset rather than a focus on what a person can get.

Understanding How People Learn: A Key to the Mentoring Mindset

In order to operate from a Mentoring Mindset, you need to understand how people learn. This will help you position your words and actions most appropriately, so your employees will gain the most from your input amd continue to grow. Most people have gaps that they are not even aware exist—until some event or individual brings them into awareness! We call this level an ***Unconscious Skill, Knowledge, Ability Gap.*** This is important to know as a leader, because it gives you the opportunity to create awareness. As you observe the gap, you can gently offer some

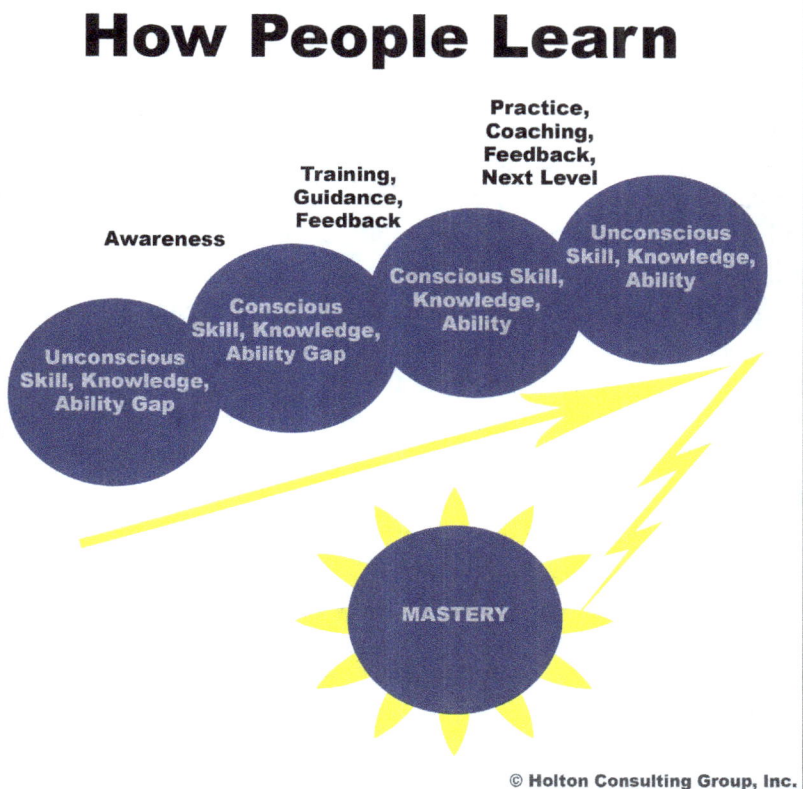

guidance or clarify a behavior that the person may not even realize they are exhibiting. This is also the stage where you can present a potential project that will require new skills, knowledge, or ability—and deal with any fears or concerns the employee may have about accepting the assignment.

Once a person recognizes the gap, it now moves into the ***Conscious Skill, Knowledge, Ability Gap***. There is a need to develop and everyone agrees on it. This is the phase where you, as a leader, can provide training, guidance, and feedback based on your own insights and experience—and suggest other appropriate avenues for development. This is also a stage where you can become an Access Provider, making necessary introductions to connect your employee with others who can be good resources.

Too often, leaders stop at this point, feeling they have done their job. But there is still more to be done, when you approach people from a Mentoring Mindset. The goal is to move the Conscious Skill, Knowledge, Ability Gap to the next level, where it becomes a ***Conscious Skill, Knowledge, Ability***. The "Gap" is removed! In other words, during this phase, you are responding to the causes of the Gap by providing ongoing coaching, feedback, and guidance to support the development of the employee. You are building confidence, encouraging growth, and increasing the ability of the employee to step out and take the initiative in the identified development area. If you have special techniques and tricks you use, this is where you can share them.

Finally, as the employee continues to practice using their skill, knowledge, ability with confidence and understanding, they move into the next level, identified as ***Unconscious Skill, Knowledge, Ability***. This is when they are able to perform without having to think about it. They intuitively use their skill, knowledge, and ability to thrive, and they are able to act on their own.

Sometimes, you get the privilege of seeing a movement into the final phase: ***Mastery***! This is when a person becomes so adept at a skill, knowledge, or ability that they move into a unique place of operating that sets them apart from the majority. A great example is someone who has learned to play the piano. Many people move to the Unconscious Skill, Knowledge, Ability phase, where they can easily pick up any piece of music and play it, adding beautiful tone and emotion to the musical score. But every now and then you experience a Mastery-level pianist, who transcends the technical aspects of playing the piano, and expresses the music with their heart and soul, moving their listeners to a whole different level of experience. Mastery is not something that can be taught; it is the absolute connection of a person's passion with the work they are doing—and it is beautiful to see! It is, quite literally, the epitomy of expression of the Extraordinary You!

As you build your own skill, knowledge, and ability in using a Mentoring Mindset, this model can be a great tool. Look for your own mentors—leaders who do a great job of creating a culture of ongoing learning and growth within their areas of operation. Seek guidance from those who do it well. Then put on your Mentoring Mindset hat and take a walk around your area. You'll be amazed at how many ways there are to help your people grow and strengthen their skills!

Strengthening Your Core Ability of a Mentoring Mindset

In addition to understanding and using the information about how people learn, here are a few other ideas of ways you can strengthen your Core Ability of a Mentoring Mindset. I promise if you put these into practice, you will experience an incredible boost in the productivity and engagement of your people, and you will wonder why you hadn't done it sooner!

- ❑ ***Get really good at listening.*** This is the key to successful leadership, in my opinion. Take classes, practice, ask for feedback on how you're doing, and never stop. You can *always* get better at listening!
- ❑ ***Get to know each of your employees.*** This goes beyond just knowing their name and job responsibilities. Dig deeper. Spend quality time with each one, to better understand their interests, their dreams, their fears, and what they need from you to do better.
- ❑ ***Practice the art of teaching empowering behavior.*** Employees reach their level of confidence in being empowered at a different rates. Your job is to lead them there, by gradually allowing them to take on more authority and responsibility. Initially you are more involved in their decision-making, so you can teach and guide them, ensuring they understand the how and why of what they are handling. As both of you grow in condidence, you can give them more and more empowerment. By the way, while this takes time initially, it eventually frees you up to do more Extraordinary Leadership kinds of things!

❏ ***Learn how to provide effective feedback.*** This is a tough one, because no one enjoys hearing anything critical about what they are doing. But as an Extraordinary Leader, you need to be able to provide both positive and constructive feedback in a way your employees are able to hear it. This takes practice! The five critical steps to ensure effective constructive feedback are outlined on the chart below.

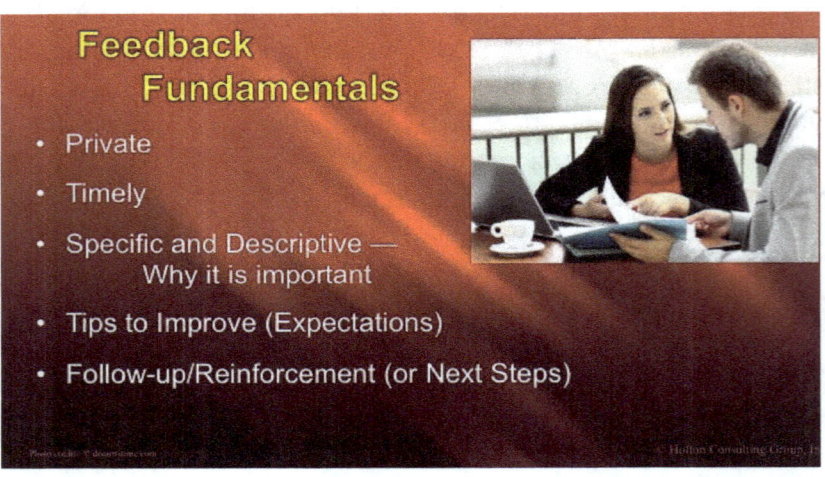

❏ ***Make positive feedback as specific and descriptive as possible.*** The more specific and descriptive, the more impact it has on the person receiving it. For example, instead of just saying, "Great job!" identify exactly what you are acknowledging: "Linda, I was so impressed with the way you handled that angry customer. You kept your cool, let him vent, and then worked with him to create a solution he appreciated. I love how he actually apologized to you! Awesome job! Thank you for representing us so well!"

❏ ***Never stop developing yourself.*** The more you strengthen your skills in leading with a Mentoring Mindset, the more ways you see to do it. Observe others who are good at it, ask your people what they need from you, get a mentor yourself, and become a perpetual learner.

The Ability & the Color: Summary

Mentoring Mindset: Recognizing that every situation can be a learning opportunity; willingly sharing your experience, insight, time, skills, and resources with all your people, knowing you are contributing to their professional growth and creating a work environment that maximizes personal/professional development, teamwork, cooperation, and engagement.

The Color Green: Green is the color representing growth and generosity. It signifies an awareness of the unending cycle of giving and receiving. Green is the color of a Mentoring Mindset because when you operate from that place of alignment, you are always on the lookout of ways to give freely, knowing that as you lead in this way you always receive more than you give. You are being true to your Core Abilities as an Extraordinary Leader!

Cultivating Your Mentoring Mindset

Too often we underestimate the power of a touch, a smile, a kind word, a listening ear, an honest compliment, or the smallest act of caring, all of which have the potential to turn a life around. (Leo Buscaglia)

Laser Focus Technique:

Preparation:

> Prepare for this Laser Focus experience by finding a quiet location where you will not be interrupted for 20 minutes.
>
> Sit in a comfortable position and take a few deep breaths, exhaling slowly between each breath. Without trying to force your breath in any way, allow it to find its own natural depth and rhythm. Always breathe through your nose. (That's assuming your nasal passages are clear and unobstructed. Otherwise breathe through your mouth.)
>
> Allow your attention to focus either on the sensation of your breath coming and going through your nostrils, or on the rising and falling of your belly as you breathe.
>
> Give your full attention to the coming and going of your breath.
>
> If you realize your attention has wandered, and you find yourself engrossed in thinking ahead to the things you need to accomplish today, or just day-dreaming, simply acknowledge it, then gently but firmly bring your attention back to your breathing.

The Process

> Think about a time when you received unexpected guidance or help from a colleague. Focus on what the situation was: perhaps you were given a project that felt overwhelming or for which you were unprepared; perhaps you were about to

make a presentation that created stress; perhaps you were about to have a difficult conversation with one of your employees. Whatever the situation, take a moment to recall how you were feeling about the difficult task you were facing.

Now take a deep breath, and recall the help your colleague provided. How was it offered? What insight did it provide for you? How did it help you as you prepared for the task ahead? How has it helped you in your professional growth as a leader?

Spend some quality time on these images. Capture the sights and sounds of your interaction with the colleague who helped you. Remember the impact his or her guidance had on your confidence level. How did integrating this advice help you during the actual event?

Now think about your employees. Imagine yourself walking through your workplace, visualizing your people involved in their tasks. Imagine observing them at work. Imagine yourself stopping to talk with each one, offering encouragement or guidance. Visualize the appreciation they express for your help, and know that the projects in your department are successfully completed.

Now focus on the following words and/or short phrases. Say each aloud three times. Do not rush through them. Speak in a normal cadenced voice:

Aware	Focused on growth
Observant	Appreciative
Good Listener	Empowering
Open-minded	Mentoring Mindset

Now, say aloud, *"I am aware."* Repeat it five times.

Say aloud, *"I am observant."* Repeat it five times.

Say aloud, *"I am a good listener."* Once again, repeat it five times.

Say aloud, "*I am open-minded.* Repeat five times.

Say aloud, *"I am focused on growth."* Repeat five times.

Say aloud, "*I am appreciative.* Repeat five times.

Say aloud, *"I am empowering."* Repeat five times.

And finally, say aloud, *"I lead with a Mentoring Mindset."* Repeat five times.

Focus once again on your hands, palms up on your lap or upper thighs. Open palms represent giving as well as receiving. So, whenever you give, you also receive. In actuality, you receive at least as much as you give. That seems to be a universal principle. As you give to your empoyees, using a Mentoring Mindset, you are receiving incredible benefits. You know this is an excellent investment of your time and energy.

When you are ready, breathe deeply and return to an awareness of your surroundings.

Self-Directed Activity to Develop Your Mentoring Mindset Core Ability: Give A Little — Get A Lot

For the next seven days, be on the lookout for every single opportunity you have to give guidance, support, information, or resources to your employees, and take advantage of it! Your giving experiences might include giving positive feedback to someone; offering to make an introduction; having coffee to discuss a project strategy; debriefing a failed project to be sure everyone learns from it; sharing some tips related to an issue someone is dealing with; helping resolve a disagreement; etc.. The list could go on and on! Your goal is to do a *minimum of one mentoring activity every day*, to develop your Mentoring Mindset.

Keep your journal handy to record not only what you did, but how you felt during this Mentoring Mindset Experiment. Also capture any unexpected benefits you receive during this time, in any form (gratitude emails, unexpected offers to buy coffee or a meal, inner feelings, new ideas related to your own projects, changes in behavior with employees, enhanced communication with another department, etc.)

At the end of seven days, use these questions to evaluate your experience:

1. How difficult was it to come up with ways to mentor every day?
2. What changes did you notice in your own emotions as the week progressed?
3. What types of benefits did you receive? How did this affect your mentoring?
4. What lessons can you take away from this activity, in terms of how you view the concept of a Mentoring Mindset?
5. How will this activity change your leadership behavior as you move forward?

Using the Color Green:

If you want to strengthen your awareness of your Mentoring Mindset, make green your color of focus. Choose to wear something green as part of your wardrobe; eat foods that are green in color (i.e., string beans, collards, peas, kale, spinach, broccoli, lima beans, kiwi, pistachio ice cream, etc.); place green in your environment (green plants, a green stone, a picture with green as the dominant color); use green ink or markers when you write.

While this may feel a little silly at first, allow yourself to give it a try without judgment. Become aware of how your Mentoring Mindset is strengthened, how you notice more opportunities for spontaneous guidance, and how your leadership is enhanced through the Mentoring Mindset.

Mentoring Mindset

Personal Reflections

*Date:*_____

Appendix

Appendix

Maximizing Your Core Abilities

Now that you're aware of the incredible power of your seven Core Abilities, it's important to recognize how to get the most benefit out of using them. Just knowing about them isn't enough, any more than owning the highest quality of golf clubs will get you on the pro tour. It's time for a little coaching—so let's go deeper.

What most people don't realize is that these Core Abilities are always present and always operating. Unless we make intentional, conscious decisions about how we are using them, they may show up in less effective behaviors that work against us.

Ineffective use of the Core Abilities can result from too little or too strong an emphasis on them. How do you achieve optimum results? I wish there was a magic wand I could give you that would guarantee success! The strength with which you use any of your Core Abilities to maximize the results is contingent on factors such as the situation, the people involved, and the urgency of the situation. This is why it is so important to understand each Core Ability to the fullest, and strengthen your ability to intentionally manage the way in which you express it. You might say you learn to use all your Core Abilities to know *how* to use all your Core Abilities in the most effective manner. Sounds a bit convoluted, I know, but it makes perfect sense.

The following chart identifies each of the Core Abilities, and describes the ineffective results of too weak or too strong a use of it. You can chart the behaviors you recognize in yourself to see where you need to put the most emphasis in your own development.

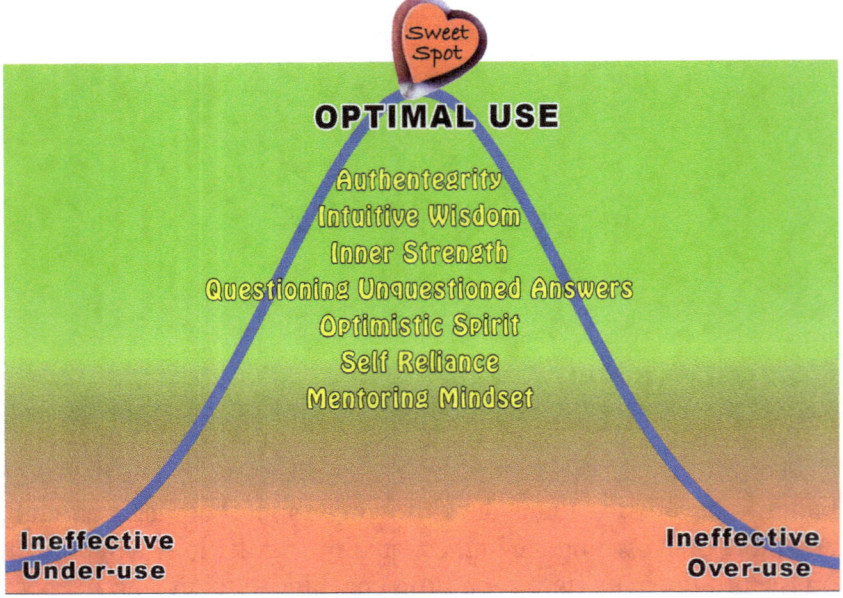

For each Core Ability listed below, the left-hand side offers examples of ineffective effects that show up from the under-use of the Core Ability; the right-hand side offers examples of ineffective effects you'll experience from the over-use of the Core Ability. Understanding these extremes can help you monitor your behavior so you can ensure you are operating from the highest, most elevated level of effectiveness with each Core Ability (the Sweet Spot).

AUTHENTEGRITY

No one trusts you
Favoritism
Changing policies for no reason

Too rigid
Harsh, Unyielding
Perfectionism

INTUITIVE WISDOM

Vacillating with decisions
Chronic regret
Second guessing yourself

Refuse to see facts
May seem "woo-woo and weird
Hard to persuade others

Appendix: Maximizing Your Core Abilities

INNER STRENGTH

Give up too soon
No initiative
Nonresilient, spiritless

Stubborn
Inflexible
Uncompromising

QUESTIONING UNQUESTIONED ANSWERS

Excessively cautious
Dogmatic
Stuck; Slow to change

Overly risk-taking
Never commit to
a firm plan
Constant change

OPTIMISTIC SPIRIT

Pessimistic
Defeated/Depressed
Negative, hard to talk to

Blind to facts
Rose-colored
glasses
Insincere

SELF-RELIANCE

Blames others
No accountability for self
Needy; Victim consciousness

Solitary
Refuse to ask for
or take help

MENTORING MINDSET

Dictatorial
Aloof; closed door policy
Unclear about expectations

Taken advantage of
Unable to provide
discipline/feedback
Takes on problems

The secret is to understand and strengthen each Core Ability so you are able to consider the situation, the individuals involved, and the urgency required, then intentionally choose the appropriate level of power to apply when using the Core Ability. That's when you hit the "Sweet Spot!" It's a constant learning process, but well worth the effort. The more effectively you use your Core Abilities, the more likely you can be an Extraordinary Leader!

Acknowledgments

No book is ever created without the help of many people! This one is no exception. The lions share of gratitude goes to my amazing husband and business partner, Bil, who is an incredible researcher, creative genius, and prolific author in his own right! He did the deep-dive into the science information that serves as a support for these Extraordinary Leadership Core Abilities, and he was my constant collaborator in developing the entire concept of this book. Bil, you are my "Person" and I thank you for your help, your support, your wisdom, your generosity, and your innumerable trips to Italian Pizzeria for dinner so I could continue to make this book a reality! You are the best!

I am also grateful to our amazing clients, who willingly served as "guinea pigs" as I shared my ideas with them. You brought the reality factor to everything I wrote about, and provided incredible examples, ideas, and feedback to this work. I am eternally indebted to you and look forward to our continued relationship.

A huge thank-you goes out to Ray Miklos, who took the risk so many years ago of hiring a young female professional to serve as the Human Resource Development Manager at Westinghouse. Ray, I am totally indebted to you for being an incredible mentor, coach, manager, and leadership model for me. You went beyond anything I ever could have learned in a book by bringing Extraordinary Leadership to life every day with your team!

Because I am so enamored by the use of color, I am appreciative to the digital agencies who compile and provide permission to use so many amazing graphics. Special thanks for the following illustration permissions (along with permission to let me do my own magic with them):

Front Cover and Title Page: clipart.com
Page 6: dreamstime.com
Page 9: clipart.com and Cher Holton

Page 12: dreamstime.com
Page 15: Cher Holton
Page 16: Bil Holton
Page 18: clipart.com
Page 21: clipart.com
Page 23: Cher Holton and clipart.com background
Page 25: graphicstock.com and Cher Holton
Page 28: iStock.com
Page 37: graphicstock.com
Page 43: Cher Holton
Page 47: clipart.com
Page 48: clipart.com
Page 59: Cher Holton
Page 60: graphicstock.com
Page 69: sxc.com
Page 73: Cher Holton and dreamstime.com background
Page 79: clipart.com
Page 87: dreamstime.com
Page 89: graphicstock.com
Page 91: dreamstime.com
Page 92: Cher Holton
Page 98: iStock.com
Page 100: Cher Holton
Page 91: sxc.com
Page 109: clipart.com
Page 119: Cher Holton and clipart.com
Page 120: clipart.com
Page 125: clipart.com and Cher Holton
Page 127: iStock.com
Page 129: graphicstock.com
Page 135: Cher Holton and dreamstime.com
Page 136: clipart.com
Page 142: Cher Holton and graphicstock.com
Page 145: clipart.com (modified Cher Holton)
Page 146: clipart.com
Page 151: Cher Holton
Page 154: Cher Holton and dreamstime.com
Page 155: dreamstime.com
Page 166: Cher Holton and wikopedia-commons
Page 181: Gaillyn Photography

Endnotes

Introduction

1. McKay, Avery, & Morris (2008). "Mean racial and ethnic differences in sales performance: The moderating role of diversity climate." *Personnel Psychology*, 61, 349-374.
2. Martin Seligman and Mihaly Csikszentmihalyi, (2000). "Positive Psychology: An Introduction," *American Psychologist* 55 (1): 5–141; William Compton, (2005). *An Introduction to Positive Psychology*. Wadsworth Publishing, pp. 1–22.
3. Andrew Newberg, *Born to Believe*, Free Press, New York, 2006.
4. Daniel Goleman, Richard Boyatzis, and Annie McKee, *Primal Leadership: Realizing the Power of Emotional Intelligence*, Teleos Leadership Institute, 2002.
5. "Blue or Red? Exploring the Effect of Color on Cognitive Task Performances," Ravi Mehta and Juliet Zhu. *Science,* Vol. 324, Issue 5915, Feb. 5, 2009; "The Impact of Color on Learning." Kathie Engelbrecht, Perkins & Will, Chicago, IL, *NeoCon 2003*, 06/18/03.
6. James, William (1890) *The Principles of Psychology*; Freud, S. *The Ego and the Id,* 1923; Jung, C. G. (1902–1905). *Psychiatric Studies. The Collected Works of C. G. Jung Vol. 1*; Maslow, A. H. (1943). "A theory of human motivation." *Psychological Review*, 50(4), 370-396; Herzberg, Frederick (1959), *The Motivation to Work*, New York: John Wiley and Sons; Skinner, B. F. (1961). "Why we need teaching machines." *Harvard Educational Review* 31: 377–398 (to name only a few).
7. Khakhria, H., *Employee Engagement Ideas to Combat the Walking Dead*, Randstad Canada, Posted on October 30, 2012.
8. Cook, M., *The New Definition of Insanity—Expecting Employee Engagement to Improve*, Human Capital League, June 26, 2013.
9. Martin Seligman, (2002). *Authentic Happiness: Using the New Positive Psychology to Realize Your Potential for Lasting Fulfillment*. New York: Free Press.

10. Schwartz, T., "New Research: How Employee Engagement Hits the Bottom Line," *Harvard Business Review*, November 8, 2012.

Chapter One—Authentegrity

1. Kernis and Goldman in Golomb, Jacob, *In Search of Authenticity*. London and New York: Routledge.
2. Goffee and Jones, "Managing authenticity: The paradox of great leadership," Harvard Business Review (12) 2005.
3. George, Ball, "What Does Authentic Leadership Really Mean?," 2016, https://www.huffingtonpost.com/bill-george-what-does-authentic-leade_b_8581814.html.
4. Farrington Partners, "Getting Real: How Authentic Leadership Benefits Business," April 30, 2015, http://farringtonpartners.com/2015/04/30/getting-real-how-authentic-leadership-benefits-business/
5. Meinecke, C., "The Problem With Authenticity," *Psychology Today*, February 22, 2013.
6. Falls, J., "The Power of Authenticity," *Convince and Convert*, July 10, 2012
7. Vossoughi, Sohrab, "How to Stand Out? Try Authenticity," *Bloomberg Businessweek*, May 28, 2008)

Chapter Two—Intuitive Wisdom

1. Faculty, *Inner Strengths of Successful Leaders Program*, Harvard Graduate School of Education, Fall 2013 Session.
2. Brown, S. C., and Greene, J. A. (2006, "The wisdom development scale: Translating the conceptual to the concrete." *Journal of College Student Development,* 47,1-19.
3. Phaedo, http://faculty.washington.edu/smcohen/320/phaedo.htm.
4. Baltes, P.B. and Staudinger, U.M. (2000). "Wisdom: A metaheuristic (pragmatic) to orchestrate mind and virtue toward excellence." *American Psychologist,* 55, 122-136

5. Sternberg, R. J. (2000). "Intelligence and wisdom." In R. J. Sternberg (Ed.), *Handbook of Intelligence* (pp. 631-649). Cambridge, England: Cambridge University Press.
6. Marchand, H. (2002). "Does wisdom increase with age?" Paper presented at 32nd Annual Meeting of the Jean Piaget Society The Embodied Mind and Consciousness: Developmental Perspectives. Philadelphia.

Chapter Three—Inner Strength

1. Quy, LaRae, http://www.laraequy.com/blog/personal-leadership/complete-beginners-guide-mental-toughness/
2. Goleman, D., *Working With Emotional Intelligence,* Bantam, New York, 1998, pg. 77.
3. Fredrickson, B., *The How of Happiness*, Three Rivers Press, New York, pg.117, 2009
4. Waugh, C., T. Wager, et al, 2008, "The neural correlates of trait resilience when anticipating and recovering from threats," *Social Cognitive and Affective Neuroscience* 3: 322- 332.
5. Faculty, *Inner Strengths of Successful Leaders Program*, Harvard Graduate School of Education, Fall 2013 Session.

Chapter Four—Questioning Unquestioned Answers

1. Elevated Labs, *Neuroplasticity and Creativity*, April 11, 2013).
2. Chopra, Deepak and Tanzi, Rudolph, *Super Brain,* Three Rivers Press, NY, 2012).
3. Guilford, J. P. , *The Nature of Human Intelligence*, 1967.
4. Kuhn, R., "What makes creative personality in business," in R. Kuhn (ed), *Handbook for Creative and Innovative Managers*, McGraw Hill, New York, 1988.
5. Chopra, D. and R. Tanzi, *Super Brain*, Random House, NY, 2012.
6. Ken Robinson's TED Conference talk, "Why schools kill creativity—The case for an education system that nurtures creativity." Monterey, California, 2006.

7. Drucker, Peter, *Innovation and Entrepreneurship,* Harper and Row, New York, 1985.
8. Kenneth M Heilman, MD, Stephen E. Nadeau, MD, and David Q. Beversdorf, MD. "Creative Innovation: Possible Brain Mechanisms" *Neurocase,* 2003.
9. Ward, T.B. (1995). "What's old about new ideas?" In S. M. Smith, T. B. Ward and R. A. and Finke (Eds.) *The Creative Cognition Approach,* 157–178, London: MIT Press.
10. Amabile, Teresa, HBS's "Teresa Amabile tracks creativity in the wild," article by Beth Potier, *Harvard Gazette,* February 10, 2005).
11. Heilman, K., *Matter of Mind: A Neurologist's View of Brain-behavior Relationships*, 2007.
12. Paris, C., Edwards, N., Sheffield, E., Mutinsky, M., Olexa, T., Reilly, S., and Baer, J. (2006). "How early school experiences impact creativity." In J. C. Kaufman and J. Baer (Eds.), *Creativity and Reason in Cognitive Development* (pp. 333-350). New York, NY: Cambridge University Press.
13. Waitley, D., *Seeds of Greatness,* Fleming Revell Company, Old Tappan, N.J., 1983.
14. Geis, G., "How risk takers take risks," in R. Kuhn (Ed), Handbook *For Creative and Innovative Mangers,* McGraw Hill, New York), 1988.
15. Pfaff, L., "Thrive in 2025: Inspire Creativity," *Parents Magazine* online post/March 2, 2013.

Chapter Five—Optimistic Spirit

1. Seligman, Martin. *Learned Optimism.* New York, NY: Pocket Books. 1998.
2. Howatt, Bill, "Why you need to be an optimistic, not pessimistic, leader." *The Globe and Mail,* (November 11, 2016).
3. Sharot T, Riccardi AM, Raio CM, and Phelps EA (2007). Neural mechanisms mediating optimism bias, *Nature,* 450 (7166), 102-5.
4. Chang, E.C., D'Zurilla, T.J., & Maydeu-Olivares, A. (1994). "Assessing the dimensionality of optimism and pessimism

using a multimeasure approach." Cognitive Therapy and Research, 18, 143-160.
5. Wiseman, Richard, *The Luck Factor*, Miramax Books, New York, 2004.
6. Sansone, C., Morf, C.C., & Panter, A.T. (Eds.) (2004). T*he Sage Handbook of Methods in Social Psychology*, Thousand Oaks, CA: Sage.
7. Achor, Shawn, *The Happiness Advantage,* Random House, New York, 2010.
8. Segerstrom, Suzanne, *Breaking Murphy's Law: How Optimists Get What They Want from Life—and Pessimists Can Too,* The Guilford Press, New York, 2006.
9. Haidt, Jonathan, *The Happiness Hypothesis*, Perseus Books Group, New York, 2006.
10. Hanson, Rick, *Buddha's Brain: The Practical Neuroscience of Happiness, Love, and Wisdom,* Oakland, Ca., New Harbinger Publications, 2009.
11. Vaughan, Susan, *Half Empty, Half Full: How to Take Control and Live Life as an Optimist,* Harvest Book, Harcourt, New York, 2000.
12. Seligman, Martin, *Learned Optimism: How to Change Your Mind and Your Life,* Pocket Books, New York, 1998.
13. Garten, Jeffrey, *The Mind of the CEO*, Basic Books, New York 2001.

Chapter Six—Self-Reliant Perspective

1. King. L. A. and Napa, C. K. (1998). "What makes a life good?" *Journal of Personality and Social Psychology*, 75, 156-165.
2. Based on test research reported by Carlson, N.R., et al. (2007). Psychology: The Science of Behaviour–4th Canadian ed., Toronto, ON: Pearson Education Canada.
3. April, K. A.; Dharani B; Peters K. "Impact of Center of Control Expectancy on Level of Well-Being." Review of European Studies 4 [2].

4. Maltby, J., Day, L., Macaskill, A. (2007). *Personality, Individual Differences and Intelligence.* Harlow: Pearson Prentice Hall)
5. Ansbacher, R. (2011). "Self-reliance, self-sufficient, sustainability." *Michigan Medicine,* 110(4), 11.
6. Siebert, Al, *The Resilliency Advantage,* San Francisco: Berrett-Koehler Publishers, 2005.
7. Mayo Clinic Staff, "Resilience: Build Skills to Endure Hardship," *Mayo Clinic Adult Health Series*, Retrieved on March 6, 2013.

Chapter Seven—Mentoring Mindset

1. Zimmerman, Lucille, *Renewed: Finding Your Inner Happy in an Overwhelmed World*, Abingdon Press, 2013.
2. Willer, R., Matthew Feinberg, Kyle Irwin, Michael Schultz, and Brent Simpson. 2010. "The Trouble with Invisible Men: How Reputational Concerns Motivate Generosity." Pp. 315-330 in *The Handbook of the Sociology of Morality*. Eds. Steve Hitlin and Stephen Vaisey. New York: Springer.
3. Grant, A., *Give and Take: A Revolutionary Approach to Success,* Viking, 2013.
4. Lyubomirsky, Sonja, *The How of Happiness*, Penguin Books, New York, 2008.
5. Fowler, J., and N. Christakris, *Connected: The Surprising Power of Our Social Networks,* Little, Brown and Company, New York, 2009
6. BlessingWhite, http://blessingwhite.com/business-issues/employee-engagement/engagement-resources, 2013.
7. Gannon, Joyce, "Mentors help reduce employees' stress and burnout," *Pittsburgh Post-Gazette,* 02/16/16.

About the Author...

Few people combine the skills of facilitator, consultant, speaker, trainer, and mentor into one dynamic bundle of energy as effectively as Cher Holton, Ph.D. Since 1984, Cher has been helping corporate and association clients enhance leadership effectiveness, employee engagement, and bottom-line results. Her Leadership Think Tank sessions, interactive keynote speeches, practical turbo-training, and unique "Retreat-Forward" team building events are practical, research-supported, and lots of fun to boot!

The programs Cher presents are deeply grounded in current leadership research, along with Positive Psychology, Neuroscience, and the Psychology of Optimism ... plus her own corporate experience in the trenches. She knows what works, and she knows how to share it! Cher is one of only a handful of professionals worldwide who has earned both the Certified Speaking Professional and Certified Management Consultant designations.

Creating customized experiences for her clients is what Cher does best. Her passion is coaching Extraordinary Leaders to build extraordinary teams, so people can be more productive, more engaged, more optimistic, and more excited about the work they do.

Cher and her husband/business partner, Bil, are co-owners of The Holton Consulting Group, Inc. They are prolific authors, perpetual learners, and ardent believers in practicing what they teach. When they aren't involved in the work they love, Cher and Bil take "Indiana Jones" vacations (such as white water rafting, sky diving, fire walking, and competitive ballroom dancing) to continually stretch their limits!

To contact Cher Holton, purchase her products, or schedule her to work with your organization or association, visit her website:
www.holtonconsulting.com

Index

A

ABCD Model 117-118
absences 18
Achor 114
Amabile 96
amygdala 111, 147
assumptions 90, 93, 94, 97, 103
Authentegrity 25-45
Authentic Self 26-27, 30-31
authenticity 25, 27, 29, 30-32, 35

B

Baltes 55-56
Bannister Effect 12
Blessing/White 150
blue 101, 106
boundaries 76
brown 79, 85
Buscaglia 154
Butler 121

C

C-Suite 118
Campbell 130
Can Guru 125
challenge 87, 103
choice 5, 34, 50, 52, 60, 74, 75, 77, 78, 105, 115, 118, 131-134, 136-138, 141-142
Chopra 89
Christakis 148
cognitive dissonance 95
Cohn 25
colors 11, 15
commitment 72, 74
complaints 18
confidentiality 33
confirmation bias 90, 93, 97
Conscious Skill, Knowledge, Ability 151-152
Conscious Skill, Knowledge, Ability Gap 151-152

contrarian opinions 33
control 70-71, 76, 81
convergent thinking 90-91
Coolidge 71
Core Nature 2, 4, 5, 7, 8, 11, 16, 22, 111, 135
creative loafing 96
Crosby 145
Csikszentmihalyi 9
customers 25, 31, 149, 150

D

Davies 10
deAngelis 29
decisions 29, 33, 34
Deeper Self 6, 7, 8, 11, 31
Deming 132
differentiation 31
Disney 92
domino effect 149
Dr. Seuss 90
Drucker 94

E

e-Engagement 3, 20, 21
e-perks 20, 21
Einstein 54, 90, 110
Einstellung Effect 91
emotional hijacking 70
Emperor's Clothes syndrome. 49
employee engagement 2, 3, 4, 9, 10, 12, 13, 14, 17, 19, 20, 21, 22, 23, 25, 72, 87, 103, 147, 149, 150, 153, 155
empowerment 84, 146, 153
externals 127-129, 133

F

facts 48, 57
Falls 30
fatigue 18
fear 57, 112, 147, 151, 153

feedback 153-154
fight-or-flight (or freeze) 90, 97, 115
Flavor of the Month 49
Ford 39
Fowler 148
Frederickson 10, 72
Fromm 7
fully present 34

G

Gallop Poll 3, 19
Garten 116, 117
Gazzaniga 10
Geiss 98
Give A Little — Get A Lot 159
givers 148
Goleman 70
Gotcha 134
Gordian Knot 98
gratitude list 76
Grant 148
Green 155, 160
Guilford 90
gut 58

H

Haidt 114
Haisch 10
Hanson 115
happiness 25, 75, 78
happiness guarantors 127
Hebbian postulate 89
Heilman 90, 97
Helmstetter 137
Horowitz 69
How is My Issue Like . . . 105

I

i-Engagement 4, 21
Inner Strength 69-85
innie 131-132
Internal Locus of Control 127

internals 127-128, 133
intrinsic motivation 96
introspection 77
integrity 25-27, 29, 31, 35, 40, 42
intrinsic motivators 17, 21
Intuitive Wisdom 47- 66

J

Jobs 73, 99
Jordan 73
Jung 25

K

knowledge 47, 54, 58, 60, 62, 90, 112
Kuhn 94

L

labels 32
Laser Focus Technique 39, 41, 61, 80, 102, 121, 137, 156
leaders 1, 2, 4, 7, 8, 12, 15, 16, 19, 21, 22, 25, 26-29, 33-34, 70-72, 74-75, 77-78, 87, 93, 95, 100-101, 104, 110, 115, 117, 123, 128-133, 136, 139, 140, 142-143, 146, 150-151-154, 155
leadership 26, 28, 30, 32, 34, 36, 38, 40, 44, 69, 70, 72, 74, 76, 78, 80, 82-86, 109, 112
Leadership "Junk-o-logic!" 49
leader logic 93
Learned Optimism 117
Lippmann 47
Lipton 10
listening 153
Lyubomirsky 10

M

mastery 152
matchers 148

Index

Mentoring Mindset 145-162
micromanage 93
Miller 7
mistakes 33, 70, 77
mood Changes 18
mystical 54, 58

N

negativity bias 112, 115, 119
neurobiology 95
neuro-hormonal chemistry 115
neuroimaging 89
neuroplasticity 89, 112
neuroscience 2, 10, 115
Newberg 7, 10, 11

O

optimalism 110
Optimistic Spirit 109-125
orange 120, 125
out-of-the-box thinking 90, 91, 93, 97, 99, 104, 106
outie 131

P

perfectionism 33, 93
Positive Psychology 2, 9
positivity 2, 10
Power of Choice 136, 137, 141
problems 88, 92, 97-98, 100, 104, 106
profitability 5
psycho-spatial processing 88, 89
purple 136, 143
Putting It Into Practice 52, 55, 75, 99, 116, 134, 149

Q

quantum physics 2
Questioning Unquestioned Answers 87-107
Quy 70

R

rational optimism 114
red 29, 37, 38
Reframe Game 116
Robinson 94
Rogers 7
rostral anterior cingulated cortex 111
Rotter 127

S

Sansone 113
Schultz 102
Segerstrom 114
Self-Reliance 127-144
self-efficacy 113
self-talk 132, 138, 139
Seligman 9, 109, 110, 117
serendipitous experiences 113
Sharot 111
Sheldon 32
Siebert 131
sociology 2
spontaneity 97
Star Player 42
Stern 7
Sternberg 55-56
stick-to-it-tiveness 77
stress 89, 90, 93, 146, 148, 155, 157
sunk-cost fallacy 34

T

takers 148
Tanzi 89
team 25, 35, 117, 124, 128, 129, 141, 142, 147, 149, 150, 153, 155.
Thompson 98
Tracy 80
True North 57

U

Unconscious Skill, Knowledge, Ability 152

Unconscious Skill, Knowledge,
  Ability Gap 150

V

values 25, 32, 34-44, 74, 78
Varghese 146
Vaughan 116
victim 128, 130-131, 136, 138
Voice From the Past 83-84
voice of eccentricity 94
Vossoughi 31

W

Weldon 97
willpower 69, 70- 71, 74
Winnicott 7
Wiseman 112
Woodman 87

Y

yellow 60, 66

www.ingramcontent.com/pod-product-compliance
Lightning Source LLC
Chambersburg PA
CBHW071438080526
44587CB00014B/1902